LISTENING EFFECTIVELY
TO CHILDREN

D1736188

BY PATTY WIPFLER

Rational Island Publishers
P.O. Box 2081, Main Office Station
Seattle, Washington 98111, U.S.A.

ISBN: 1-58429-036-6

$7.00

TABLE OF CONTENTS

Introduction .... *i*

Special Time 1

Playlistening 11

Crying 29

Tantrums and Indignation 43

Healing Children's Fears 55

Reaching For Your Angry Child 77

INTRODUCTION

Congratulations! You are one of the very fortunate parents who have happened upon Re-evaluation Counseling and its insights about how people thrive and heal. You will appreciate your good fortune daily. You now have access to dependable insights that will help you convey your love and caring to your children and let you lift distresses from their lives. Your pleasure in your life as a mother or a father has a chance to grow and deepen with time, as discharge works to clear away confusion and increase your power as a loving parent and community-builder. This is the kind of power that every parent hopes for!

The key insight around which our approach to children is built is that children thrive when they feel connected. From infancy forward, a child's need for significant human connection with many other people is as strong as the need for food, sleep, and shelter. You can see infants drink in the loving gaze of their father or mother with long, unwavering looks. You can see a young child's whole body light up with hope when a loved one calls her* name. You can hear the good clear ring of laughter when a child feels safe in play with her friends. These moments of connection are what carry a young child's confidence from challenge to challenge in a world that she doesn't fully understand and can't fully command.

---

*In order to simplify the text, the pronoun "she" or "he" is used to refer to children of both genders.

The confidence a child feels in herself, her abilities, and her loved ones is strong. Most of us have a difficult time recalling what life can be like when we are buoyed high with the hope that "today will be great!" This confidence is our children's birthright, and ours as well.

This confidence stands behind children's great capacity for learning, their willingness to experiment, their creativity, and their directness. In a sense, *they know themselves, they know their intelligence,* and they don't have to stop to question or censor themselves as they explore their world and their relationships. This confidence is deep, it is precious. It is worth great effort to preserve our children's confidence in themselves and in us.

To do this, you can use the information that follows to build your ability to connect, and to reconnect, with your child. Distress and restimulation fray the connections, but our situation is full of hope. Our children persistently reach out for connection, so we're not alone in taking initiative. They let us know when they've been hurt, so it's not hard to see when to get down to work. And they shine so readily when we manage to figure out how to be helpful toward them.

In developing these understandings of how the insights of Re-evaluation Counseling work with young children, we parents bumbled back and forth between getting discharge for ourselves in sessions and trying to listen to and understand our children's bids for attention. Although the information about counseling children on their distresses is pretty well organized at this point, our learning process was not! What we learned seemed to be driven either by what distresses our children were bringing up most persistently, or by what distresses they had that we could least abide. In any case, "Discharge, discharge, discharge" turned out to be Answer Number One to most of the questions we had. So as you start to use these ideas, don't worry about whether you are making lots of mistakes (you are if you're learning!) or whether it seems hard. It will feel hard. The thinking you and your child recover will be well worth the effort.

The difficulties you feel will stem from two sources: the rigid patterns that your family passed on to you, and the harshness of the oppression of parents. The rigidities from your family will, with the help of other RCers, be fairly straightforward to tackle in sessions. You'll have a chance to grow patient in ways your parents couldn't, to express caring in tones you never heard yourself, to play lightly in ways you never could as a child, with your Co-Counselors leading you where those you grew up with could not lead.

The oppression of parents in our society means that your efforts to support your child and to *connect* in relationships rather than *control* will restimulate some people. Already a target for criticism, as all parents are, you will need to learn to handle the distresses of people in your family, your neighborhood, and your circle of friends. They will notice a kind of attention toward children that they haven't seen before, and you will make parenting decisions they don't understand. The simple act of trying to use a set of clear ideas about children will trigger upset in some corners. Try not to let these upsets confuse you. Keep discharging, learning, communicating your thinking, and trusting that people are good.

As a parent, you are entitled to learn, to think, to try things, to test ideas. Every parent does this, consciously or not. You will not know what to do many times a day, and you will also do things with "confidence" that will turn out to be misguided. There is no way to learn to be with children well without this kind of messiness. The set-up of parents' oppression takes away from you the time and energy to do this learning in relation to your child and the institutions you and your child deal with. The society is set up to "advise you," "admonish you," and keep you isolated from other parents' best thinking. At bottom, it is set up to ignore the nurturing of your child and of your parenting efforts, treating this most vital stage of loving and living as though it counted for nothing and your real life would begin as soon as you "get back to work." Your work with your child makes a future for all society, but there's no making a profit from it this year, so in the oppressive society, it doesn't "count."

Against the pull of this way of seeing things, you'll do well to set up a parents' support group which can help remind you of the importance of your work as a mother or father. The connections we have within our families are precious. The things we learn as we pay attention to our children can be profound and can make the rest of our lives much more powerful. The gaps in our intelligence that our children help us identify are well worth attending to. And mothers and fathers are a joy to be with. There is great good in working together as human beings on the project of attending to our children's needs, and to our needs as their nurturers.

SPECIAL TIME

LISTENING TO CHILDREN WITH "SPECIAL TIME"

We parents love our children! Our love for them is often the most deeply felt emotion we have ever experienced. We may not always find it easy to express this love, but it is certainly a powerful force in our lives! The times when we can relax, play, and connect with our children are at the heart of our precious relationship with them. But relaxed time for parent and child to share their love is always in short supply. Both parents and children long for more.

Parents are not at fault for this short supply of easy time. In our society, the work of parenting is sadly undervalued and poorly understood. Most parents plan for warmth and closeness within their families but find themselves saddled with enough responsibility to occupy three full-time people. Overwork separates us from our children. We patch our family life together with full hearts but with few tools and very little help. Long range, a major task of our society will be to provide mothers and fathers with the tools and help they need to support the important work they do as parents. We should aim to make it possible for parents to enjoy their children and their parenthood without constant worries about survival.

The practice of giving "special time" to your child is an excellent tool for parenting in difficult times. It is a simple yet powerful way of building and strengthening

1

close relationships with our children. It can also be an antidote to those feelings of "not being a good enough parent" that plague us and spoil our enthusiasm. When we make the time to fully concentrate on our relationships with our children, we satisfy some of the deep needs for loving and being close that are natural to people of every age. We begin to take fuller pride in our parenting. Our children thrive on our growing confidence as parents, and on the attention we give them.

In particular, "special time" is a way of creating the safe relationship your child needs with you to fully discharge any hurts or confusions she* has collected in her life so far. When you focus your attention completely on her, you invite her to rely on you as her counselor. Your child's play becomes her vehicle for telling you about her life and perceptions.

To begin, you focus your entire attention on your child. This is not casual play or indirect contact! Decide to notice everything about your child's words, expression, tone of voice, posture, and movement. Absorb information through your every pore, as if your child were entirely new to you! Here are further guidelines for setting up "special time":

- Set aside a short, defined period of time during which there will be no interruptions at all: no telephone, no doorbell, no siblings to be tended, no cups of tea to be made, no need for you to do anything except be with your child. (You can use a timer if you wish, to show that you will protect this time between you.)

- Do what you can to be free of worries and fatigue. Choose a time when you are able to take a deep breath, leave the dishes in the sink, and spend time enjoying the remarkable child you have brought into your family.

- During "special time," *put your child in charge* of her relationship with you. Let your child know that, for this time period, you are willing to do anything she wants. Follow her lead, whether she tells you or simply shows you what she wants to do. This reversal of the usual balance of power between you will encourage your child to bring up thoughts and feelings she cannot entrust to you in the everyday bustle of family life. You are contradicting the conditions of young people's oppression.

- Let her know you are enjoying her thoroughly. Let your affection, interest, and approval show on your face, in your voice, and through your touch. Your child may seem to ignore your added warmth, but don't stop and wait for gratitude or a return of your affection. Your child will absorb your caring and will decide how to use it in her own time and way.

- Expect new things to happen. Your tone of expectation and interest will help your child make use of this opportunity to show you new things about herself. To be a good counselor, you must make no assumptions about what will happen during this time.

- Don't give in to the temptation to direct the play with your own ideas or to "teach" how it could be done "better." Your child needs many opportunities to use her own judgment and to experiment freely. The modifications to play that you suggest will keep you from fully understanding *her* ideas, *her* preferences, and *her* enthusiasms. Modify the play only if what your child suggests is clearly unsafe.

AS YOU LISTEN, YOUR CHILD'S TRUST IN YOU WILL BUILD

When you give your child "special time" on a regular basis, she'll build a deeper trust in you. She will show you more of herself, how she sees the world, and how she feels. You will probably see some of the following developments (not necessarily in this order), which will indicate that your child is feeling safer with you.

- **You may be tested.** Your child may choose to do the kind of play you find most boring or most irritating, to see if you really will be delighted with her "no matter what." This may mean that you will be asked to learn to roller skate, or to play video games, or to splash lots of water in the kitchen sink. You may need to discharge in your own sessions about what you don't like about the play your child chooses, so that you can think about what your child is trying for and how to respond flexibly. When you can be enthusiastic about your child's choice of play during "special time," trust will increase rapidly.

- **Your child may explore new activities or new territory with your attention.** A child will often decide to use the safety of adult attention to test her physical limits by jumping on beds in every possible way, or walking down the block farther than ever before, or putting every possible item, including herself, into a large mud puddle. She will use your permission and approval to do intensive, whole-bodied learning.

- **Your child will show you issues of importance.** Your open enjoyment and relaxed attitude will sooner or later invite your child to try to face issues which challenge her. For instance, if your child has recently been given a painful shot at the doctor's office, you may find yourself the recipient of vigorous shots gleefully given during "special time." Or if a teacher has scolded her, she may play "teacher" and scold you with the same words and tone. She is using the play to set up an opportunity for discharge on a distress she thinks you can help her with. Your offer to listen to her has been energetically accepted.

- **Your child will bring up a wide variety of issues.** The safety of "special time" will give your child permission to show you details of her thinking and distresses around power, violence, medical treatment, physical pain, her body, separation, eating, a collection of occasional fears, and more. She will use listening time from you to discharge on these issues through play, talk, and outbursts of feelings.

- **Your child may show an increasing attachment to you.** Your child will discover that having "special time" with you is deeply reassuring. You will notice positive changes in her: increased affection, hopefulness, excitement about life, sharing of thoughts, and accomplishments. Your child notices these changes too, and will want more of your attention to help her feel good about herself. Her bids for your attention may become more frequent throughout the day. She may feel safe enough to show you feelings of dependency or nameless fears which have lingered from infancy, such as being afraid of the dark again. This may look like a "regression" to "more immature" behavior and will probably be quite irritating to you at first. In actuality, this is progress. Your child has used the trust built during "special time" to dare to show you troubles she has been carrying alone. She is now able to ask for your help to resolve these important issues.

- **Old difficulties which you thought your child had resolved are likely to reappear.** When children try to show their difficulties to their parents and are distracted, ignored, reprimanded, or isolated, they eventually give up trying to get help and adopt some repetitive behavior or ritual to keep themselves from feeling so bad on difficult occasions. Given increased safety in your relationship, your child may decide to get your listening help with this unfinished business. She will not confine her requests for listening time to "special time" but will simply begin to complain, tantrum, or cry when things upset her. From your child's point of view, she feels sure of your acceptance, so the discharge process is at her fingertips.

THE "PLAYLISTENING" RESPONSE TO CHILDREN'S ISSUES

One of the basic keys to counseling a child is an active way of responding which is quite different from what we think of as ordinary play. "Playlistening" is a kind of listening in which you demonstrate your willingness to see what your child thinks and feels by clearly giving him the powerful role in play. When you take upon yourself the smaller, weaker, less competent role, your child feels confident enough to *show* you his thoughts and feelings around important issues. As counselor, you look for opportunities to help your child discharge his tensions around a particular issue through laughter as you play.

Let's use the example of the child who wants to give Daddy a shot (having been given one recently himself). He has shown Daddy the distress. If Daddy, putting aside his usual composure, can playfully squirm and try to get away, or playfully yelp and tell the child in comic-opera fashion, "No! No shot! Help!" then the child can laugh and persist in doing to Daddy what he feels was done to him. It's often possible for a child to laugh extensively if the adult will lightly play the helpless role and allow the child the powerful role.

This playful role reversal lets the child continue to be in charge of the relationship. He is in charge of unfolding his feelings and perceptions around the issue. His laughter dissolves significant tensions around that issue: a child can continue to laugh for half an hour or longer, if the adult can keep playing that long. A game that begins with lots of laughter around giving shots to Daddy, who tries in vain to get away, might later turn into making loud noises at Daddy, who jumps in exaggerated fear, and then might gradually move toward throwing a pillow at Daddy to make him fall down every time he struggles to his hands and knees, all with much laughter and glee.

To begin playlistening, notice what allows your child to laugh and do more of whatever that may be. A good playlistener will act helpless enough to be non-threatening, but active enough to be interesting. He will keep his attention on what the *child* shows about the issue. For example, if your child wants you to chase him, don't assume that you should chase him as a "monster." (We adults have the strong tendency to change the entire subject of a child's play to fit our own ideas.) If a chase is called for, simply chase your child with noisy effort but little success. You might catch his shirttail for a moment, or you might succeed in tackling him (look for what brings the most laughter), but he always gets away in the end. On the other hand, if your child *says* he wants you to be a monster, play a befuddled, stumbling, incompetent monster, not a large and threatening one.

When a child is very small, adults need to play a very helpless role to contradict his powerlessness and allow him to laugh. As a child grows in strength and self-assurance, he needs fuller resistance and more of a contest to keep the laughter rolling. A child will screech frantically if you are being too forceful in play because his fears have made him unsure of your good intentions. Slow down and become less competent if your child is screeching rather than laughing, so he can regain the initiative. He needs to feel fully safe and in charge in order to discharge on a distress through laughter. Another caution: don't tickle. Tickling is a form of unaware touching which can easily victimize children.

Parents sometimes worry that if they playfully take the less powerful role, their child will lose respect for them. This worry is unfounded. However, your child *will* become thrilled with the opportunity to show you his issues and struggles in this non-painful way and will probably want far more playlistening than you feel prepared to do. After a playtime with lots of laughter, your child may be obviously affectionate, close, and relaxed. Sometimes deeper feelings will flow more freely. Tiny difficulties can easily bring on a long, hearty cry after a playtime full of laughter. The play and laughter have thoroughly reassured your child. Now he is using that reassurance to discharge more deeply on his distresses.

Playing actively and non-threateningly with children doesn't come easily to most of us. Generally, our parents were working too hard and under too many pressures to play this way when we were children. We have not had much exposure to adults who can set aside their worries and play actively without having to dominate. Taking time in your own sessions to discharge on the irritations and worries that prevent you from playing will help you keep experimenting despite your discomforts.

LISTENING TO A CHILD'S DEEPER FEELINGS

Both adults and children search for friendships in which there is enough safety to allow feelings to accompany the thoughts we express. Our closest relationships are usually with people who love us enough to let us show how we feel, without hurrying us toward composure. Children show deep feelings easily: tantrums in frustration, the perspiration and trembling that accompany fear, and lots of crying when there is grief. Children of parents who listen well will cry and rage frequently during their childhood, as the discharge process clears away tensions and confusions. A child's fears and griefs are like unwanted baggage: they require much of a child's attention if they must be managed and carried along. But if the child can fully reveal and unload them, he is free to be his loving, confident, cooperative self again.

It is very useful to a child to be allowed to continue discharging feelings until the feelings subside. Our typical reaction to our child's show of feelings is to "do something quick" to help him regain his composure. We adults worry that the child has plunged into irrationality and might never recover a balanced perspective. In fact, the opposite is true: discharging feelings will dependably improve a child's perspective and confidence when an adult who has decided to be counselor provides basic caring, reassurance, and respect.

When tears or tantrums begin, it is important that a parent gently continue to listen, thoughtfully staying near the child, touching him or holding him gently, and saying a few words of caring. For example, "Tell me more," "I love you," "I'm sorry it happened that way." If you say too much, you'll dominate the interaction, and you won't be listening anymore. Your child will feel deeply cared about if you are able to listen to how he feels without trying to "correct" his feelings. When a child has stormed or cried the feelings through, he will begin to notice you and his surroundings again and will generally feel deeply relieved and refreshed. Light laughter or yawns will often follow a stormy cry, indicating that a child is re-evaluating and gaining an improved perspective.

When a child feels tense or isolated, he may "set up" a situation so that an adult will have to set limits on his behavior. Once reasonable limits have been set, the child takes the opportunity to cry or rage and can release the tension he has been feeling. If allowed to discharge his upset with some reassurance and good listening, the child will emerge from the outburst relaxed, relieved, warm, aware, and reasonable, accepting of the limits that were set. However, if there is a large backlog of tension, anger, or mistrust, your child may need to cry or rage extensively several times before he is able to clear away enough emotional debris to remember that he is loved and cherished.

Many parents find that counseling a child through his tears or tantrums, without putting demands on him to "pull himself together," is actually much easier and more rewarding than trying to control, distract, or force polite behaviors upon him. Times of tears and rage are times which you can very effectively communicate your love for your child, who feels that his world has fallen apart. When you stay close, without demands, he can put his world back together in his own good time, with your caring as an active part of the picture. He will feel deeply loved when you have continued to show that you care through the worst of his feelings.

Giving your child regular "special time" will start you on the path of respecting your child's judgment and helping him with the distresses he is eager to shed. This kind of listening is at first extremely difficult for almost all parents! Most of us didn't receive the kind of care and listening we are learning to give. In this uncharted territory, we are bound to feel uncomfortable at times. But our children's response can be our guide. Every time we listen well through their tears, every time a "special time" is full of exploration or laughter, they'll show us that we're strengthening the bonds of love and trust we want to build with them.

PLAYLISTENING

GROWING CLOSER TO YOUR CHILD
THROUGH LAUGHTER

Children love to laugh. The more they can laugh, the livelier they become. They delight in themselves and their partners in play. Children feel safe and understood when adults relax, get close, and let free play and laughter begin. Drawing out our children's laughter is great for us, too. Their full-bodied giggles are one of the real joys of parenting. Our lives often go better when we pursue the simple pleasures of giving horsie rides, playing chase, and catching our leaping children as they fling themselves from the back of the sofa into our arms.

There is a particular way of playing with children that can provide great fun and at the same time help them resolve some of their hesitancies, fears, and worries. It is child-guided play, in which you take a role that builds your child's confidence and resilience through laughter. The point of this play is to make affectionate, lively contact with your child, with your guarantee that her pride won't be dashed. This play is one of the main skills we can develop as counselors of our children. I call it "playlistening."

To your child, playlistening looks and feels like play of the most wonderful kind! Your role is to give your child the upper hand, allowing her to be safely in charge, while you maintain moment-to-moment awareness of her initiatives and her responses. You look for ways to play that let her laugh extensively, without changing the content of the play she has chosen. In our competitive society, play often turns into a contest to determine who is "better." Playlistening is a time when the adult ensures that any contest will be lively, and will be won by the superior strength and cleverness of the *child*. Although we and our children intuitively set up play that includes laughter now and again in our daily lives, understanding this kind of play and how to initiate it can bring a lighter touch to our parenting, and help our children feel thoroughly loved. It's a tool we can use to grow closer to our children, help them resolve the issues that concern them, and build their self-assurance.

PLAYFULLY TAKE THE LESS POWERFUL ROLE

Playlistening begins any time you allow your child to take the powerful role in play, casting yourself in the role of the smaller, slower, less competent one. Your child is clever, and you are dim-witted. Your child is strong, and you are weak. Your child is graceful, and you are clumsy. Your child is bold, and you are shy. The idea is not to try to act childishly, but to lightheartedly adopt a less competent role. You're not trying to fool anyone about your real capabilities. You're not giving up your parental responsibilities. You're offering your child a bit of relief from the rigors of childhood, which include being smaller, weaker, less respected, less skilled, and less free to determine how life goes. The laughter that results when your child finds herself more powerful than you will release significant tensions. It will also bring you both closer.

For example, perhaps a child wants Daddy to push her on the swings at the park. Daddy pushes her from the front, so he can shower her with affection and approval. In response to his extra warmth, she shoves him with her foot as he pushes. Daddy, putting aside his usual composure, jumps in mock surprise and fear. She laughs heartily. Now, every time he leans toward her, she gives a little shove, and poor befuddled Daddy yelps and jumps away, "Hey! What in the world was that? Did I feel something?" He asks her innocently, "Did your foot touch my tummy?" She laughs and pretends to know nothing, so he says, "Well, I'm just going to swing you and love you!" He greets her warmly again and again, and she laughs heartily as she plays at fending off his affection with little shoves that "scare" and "confuse" him.

AS PLAYLISTENING CONTINUES, SPECIFIC ISSUES MAY UNFOLD

This playful role reversal puts the child in charge of the relationship and lets her determine how the play goes. In the counselor role, the adult is contradicting the lack of power in young people's lives. In the example above, all the father did to get things started was to show more warmth than usual and to take the less powerful role when his child responded. We can only guess what distresses children are discharging in their laughter. Perhaps this child was dissolving some of her embarrassment about receiving affection. Perhaps she was laughing as the tension of having a usually serious, overworked Daddy was melting away. We do know that when children direct playlistening, they soon focus the play to suit their own agendas. Often, they will shift the play toward specific distresses they hope to discharge.

For instance, from this play on the swing the child in the park might start to make loud noises at Daddy, who obligingly startles in exaggerated fear. She laughs and scares him over and over. Then she hops off the swing and runs toward him, tackling him to the ground in her most daring move yet. She giggles happily as he tries to crawl away, calling feebly for help. She pushes him to the ground many times with great laughter and energy, growing bolder physically and verbally. Pretty soon she's telling him, "If you don't do what I say, I'm going to lock you out of our room!" in the exact words and tone her big brother uses when he is upset with her at home. She has outlined a specific distress: the incident in which she was threatened by her brother. If Daddy responds by playfully protesting, perhaps pounding his fists on the grass and saying, "Don't *do* that to me!" or affectionately boxing her tummy, protesting, "No way! I won't let you lock me in!" she can laugh extensively. She is reenacting the power struggle she has lost so many times before and is discharging her way toward confidence as she "wins" in play.

LAUGHTER HEALS CHILDREN'S TENSIONS

The healing power of playlistening lies in the laughter the child does. Embarrassments, light fears, and timidities dissolve. A playtime full of laughter fills a child with hope. It creates a strong sense of closeness and understanding between children and the adults who play with them. Children can continue laughing and elaborating on issues for an hour or more if an adult is willing. Both general and specific distresses a child carries are addressed in the play and relieved through laughter. You won't always understand what tensions your child is undoing as she plays, but you will see positive changes in her afterward.

For instance: a six-year-old I know was very reluctant to write or learn the alphabet. He seemed to want nothing to do with pre-reading skills. He felt badly about himself when forced to write, as his skills were not up to par. He was in a play group in which there were several adults who would playlisten as much as the children wanted. It was always his choice to roughhouse and chase, jumping on the adults and "getting" them, then laughing intensely as they tried to "get" him back. The play was fast and vigorous, and he was at his most creative as he invented surprise captures and daring getaways.

After a long period of nonstop action with lots of wrestling, laughter, and perspiration, he would relax, catch his breath, and get a drink. Then he would ask his adult buddy to go to the blackboard, where he would (without prompting) concentrate on mastering the alphabet. After these playtimes, both his attention span and his tolerance for his own mistakes were great. We didn't know what the issues were that he was working through, but *he* certainly knew how to direct the play to overcome his fears and to use his newfound confidence to tackle an important challenge.

CHILDREN HUNGER FOR PLAYLISTENING

Once you see the delight and vigor with which children engage in playlistening, you begin to get a sense of their hunger for this kind of attention from adults. Children make immediate use of play that lets them laugh away the distresses they collect as small people in a large and fast-paced world. They treasure the adults who will romp with them, follow their lead, and let them laugh.

HOW TO BEGIN

To begin playlistening, simply notice what lets your child laugh, and do more of it. You might, like the father swinging his daughter, begin by being playfully warm. Pick up on your child's cues, finding some pretext which will let you affectionately assume the less powerful role. For example, in a game of hide-and-seek, instead of being an adept finder, you could tromp around loudly, get closer, and finally grope all over your child's feet without seeing her. Or if she wants to play a board game, when your roll of the dice is disappointing, you could moan and tug on her arm, begging her to let you roll again. None of your work associates are likely to walk through the door as you play, so you are free to experiment with being undignified. Your child will love your growing ability to bumble and beg.

Opportunities to playlisten are frequent. Any giggle opens the door. At my day care center one day, a caregiver was having a good time singing with the toddlers. She got up and crossed the room to open the window, tripping slightly on a crease in the carpet. She heard a few giggles behind her and took her cue from eight little people deeply interested in the art of walking and running. She turned in mock indignation, saying lightly, "Who's that laughing at me? I can walk just fine! Watch me!" They watched in delight as she crossed the room and tripped again. Lots of laughter this time. "Oh dear! Well, I guess I have to try again. Here I go." She tripped many more times, trying with great exaggeration to walk gracefully, which elicited a steady ripple of laughter. Eventually, several of the toddlers began running across the room, falling on their tummies and giggling, delighted with themselves and their friends. At last, they weren't the only ones having trouble walking! They were bursting with enjoyment and relief.

BASIC GUIDELINES FOR PLAYLISTENING

As you experiment, you will find ways to make playlistening your own tool. Here are a few general guidelines that may help you elicit healing laughter from your child without dominating the play.

• **Make physical contact. Be actively affectionate.**

There's nothing quite as reassuring to a child as the feel of a person who loves her. Most of the contact we make with children is gentle or practical in nature: combing their hair, buttoning their shirts, kissing them goodbye on the cheek. When a loving parent affectionately and actively pursues his child, lots of laughter often breaks out.

Nuzzling, enthusiastic cuddling, rolling together on the floor, romping, and wrestling all are great fun for children.

A word needs to be said about safety, though. A child feels safe with physical play if the adult seeking contact is aware of the child's wishes at all times. Children will run away and love to be caught and hugged again and again, but only if the adult is playing flexibly and not trying to fill some pre-set need for love or approval from the child. As soon as the play turns into an earnest contest to see who can control what the child does, she will stop feeling safe. Indeed, it won't really be play anymore.

- **Be sure not to overwhelm or overpower your child.**

Your goal is to keep your child feeling delighted and triumphant. It is marvelous to see her this way! To strike the right balance between challenge and success, the adult must be sensitive to nuances of the child's response, on a second-by-second basis. If you are being too forceful, a child will laugh frantically or screech. Try not to push a child to this panicky edge of her fears. Some children are quite unsure of themselves, and for them subtle things such as moving too close or moving too quickly can stop the laughter. If you see signs of fear, take a less forceful approach in order to keep the play safe. Play more slowly, bumble more often. A good listener will act helpless enough to be non-threatening but active enough to be interesting and will keep his attention on how the child unfolds the issues.

In particular, don't tickle. Tickling is not affectionate or helpful to children. A child being tickled is not in control at all, and it can be quite frightening because her laughter prevents her from saying she wants the tickling to stop. Many adults who were mercilessly tickled as children now find it difficult to relax while being physically close.

We must not overwhelm children by tickling them or jabbing at them, even though laughter seems to be a result.

• **Tailor the strength of play to your child.**

When children are very small, adults need to play a very helpless role to help them laugh. To elicit laughter when a toddler touches your shoulder, you collapse on the floor with a groan. As children grow in strength and self-assurance, they need fuller resistance and more of a contest to keep the laughter rolling. Young people who feel strong and competent will laugh more fully if you put up a vigorous struggle before you are out-run or out-wrestled. They want to be tested but they still need to know that with you, they won't lose.

Children, both girls and boys, love rough-and-tumble play, unless they have been made to feel weak or afraid. As play with laughter continues, a child builds courage and confidence. You will see that after fifteen or twenty minutes of your allowing your child the upper hand, she will play more boldly, more deftly than before. Your role in the play will need to change as your child's initiative changes. It takes real skill to fine-tune your attention to the details of her play so that she continues to be challenged in a way that sparks her interest and unleashes her laughter.

• **Don't let your own distresses intrude.**

Sometimes, because of the distresses we've acquired in childhood, we will tend to direct the play toward issues the child did not raise. Perhaps your child asks to be chased. The play is quite lively, full of giggles, for awhile. Every time you reach for her, she gets away, laughing and pleased with herself. Then, for some reason, you begin to say, "I'm the Monster from the Green Lagoon. Arrrgh!" You enjoy the play more as you smack your lips and make scary sounds, stomping through the house and breathing loudly. After a time, you notice her staring at you from a corner with a serious, frightened look. Oops! The monster was your idea, and it made the play unsafe. Back to the chase your child designed.

It's not easy to follow a child's lead in play. We have our own preferences, and the issues our children choose to work on aren't always ones we're comfortable with. In fact, sometimes children will, with their marvelous intelligence, choose to explore kinds of play they know their parents don't like. I think it's their way of inviting us to work on our own distresses. For instance, my sons' favorite laughing game for a while was to have me lie on the carpet, with them standing high above me on the back of the sofa. One at a time, they would jump down, as if to land with both feet on my poor stomach. At the last split second, their feet would part, and they'd land on the floor instead. I would laugh and squirm and wonder loudly (and only half-jokingly) if I was going to live. In the hundreds of jumps they took, they never hurt me. I figure they gave me lessons in bravery and trust that I would not have otherwise chosen.

When you are uncomfortable with the play your child chooses, and there is no real danger involved, her laughter will begin to roll if you playfully exaggerate your discomfort. "Oh no! You're going to jump from the sofa! Oh, please—you're my only daughter! What if the mattress on the floor doesn't save you! My precious girl! What about your beautiful knees! Your sweet forehead! Do you really **have** to jump?" If you create a cartoon of your worries, both you and your child will laugh and be challenged.

- **When a limit needs to be set (and the situation isn't dangerous), try setting it playfully with playlistening.**

Children will test limits because they are tense, or because they are feeling separate from everyone. Playlistening can often dissolve this tension, giving the child enough affection, contact, and discharge to remind her that she belongs and is loved.

There are lots of playful, light-as-a-feather tones in which to say "No." The trouble is, few of us ever heard these tones, and we can't imagine a "No" without some threat or harshness behind it. Try experimenting with the pitch of your voice, your words, and some exaggerations of grown-up, serious "No" to see if you can discover your talent in this department. I like to use an exaggerated "Uh-oh! You're in trouble now!" said with great affection, or a high-pitched "Oohhh! How could you do that!" in enthusiastic protest. You can chase slowly after the young offender, finally nuzzling her or pulling her into a vigorous cuddle. Always, with a humorous "No," affection and playful contact should follow to bring the play to laughter and tension release for the child.

The playful "No" addresses the tension that causes a child to test limits, and it communicates acceptance. It's not the only appropriate response to a child who is testing, of course, but it's a powerful builder of closeness and understanding. Adding the playful "No" to your relationship lets a child safely show you over and over again what forbidden things she would like to do, and to laugh the tension away. For example, as your child reaches for her brother's prized robot, you swoop down, scoop her into your arms, and run jauntily with her into the next room. She laughs, wiggles away, and heads for the robot again. You catch her playfully just before she gets there. Over and over, she can laugh as she shows you how much she wants that special robot. You give her affection and vigorous contact instead. Often, after such a playtime, a child can cry heartily in your arms about not wanting to play the game anymore but *really* wanting the forbidden item. This relieves more of the distress which has glued her desire onto something she can't have. She'll be free to remember pleasures other than that robot when her tears and laughter have restored her better judgment. Playlistening "No" can make your limit-setting duties much more interesting. The opportunity for creative problem-solving is greater when you have humor and lightness in your toolbox.

• **Put your "dignity" on the shelf and be active.**

Children are reassured by adult enthusiasm. In playlistening, you'll almost always eventually be asked to play full-out. Trail around after your two-year-old on hands and knees. (Kneepads make this easier!) Let your ten-year-old chase you down the stairs. Run playfully screeching from the room when your five-year-old jumps out from behind the door to scare you. The more fully you can move, the more original your children will be as they make games that let them laugh and grow more confident.

HEALING SPECIFIC DISTRESSES WITH PLAYLISTENING

When you see that your child is caught in repetitive, isolating behavior, you may be able to use playlistening to lift the tension that has trapped her. Children dangle repetitive behavior such as thumbsucking and whining in front of us, hoping that we will help them. They would much rather play constructively, but they've fallen into a lonely little rut and don't know how to get themselves out. When you approach a child in a warm and playful manner, she often can use your attention to laugh her way back into contact with you, then into flexible play again.

For a child who is thumbsucking with a blank gaze, a little playlistening adds the warmth and contact she needs to help her engage in life again. Try playfully nuzzling her, nibbling her hair or her ears, or bouncing kisses up her tummy. She'll stop sucking her thumb as soon as your invitation to play has been persistent enough. If her passivity covers some sadness, she may cry instead of laugh when you give her your active attention. But whether she goes for tears or for laughter, your unshakable affection will help her discharge the feelings that keep her disengaged.

A whining child can also be nudged into healing tears or laughter if you bring her closeness and warmth in a playful way. We are sometimes tempted to mock a child who is whining—to whine back or deride her. This is not helpful. When your child is moaning helplessly, "I wanna cooookie," you can sidestep the request entirely and instead address the fact that she is feeling far away. Look cheerfully at her and say, "And *I* want a nibble of your ear," and begin jauntily planting kisses up her arm toward her ear. Or merrily scoop her up, hold her in your arms, and march through the house with her, chanting, "We want a cookie! We want a cookie!" looking for the places where laughter can break through because you are being so silly.

In both examples above, you are approaching a child who feels out of kilter, and most importantly, out of touch with you. (Children can feel this way even in the midst of lots of adult attention.) You bounce into her world with affection and a light tone, searching for the giggle that will begin to rebuild her sense of closeness and belonging. What you do and say as you bounce doesn't have to make much sense. It's your affectionate, happy-go-lucky tone that will carry the day. This is, for us, a much more interesting and independent way to respond to a child's difficulty than the traditional "I want you to stop that right now." A humorous response is, in a way, our refusal to climb into a child's unhappy little rut with her. When we decide to respond with warmth, we reach for the little person we know and love. Often, we find her and create a good time for us both.

As you experiment with playlistening, try inventing ways to help your child with specific fears, too. When you see that she's afraid to learn to swim, you can snuggle up to her, give her an expectant look, touch your toe to the water at the edge of the pool, and kick your foot high with a frightened yelp. She'll find a way to laugh, perhaps by forcing your foot back into the water so you'll kick and yelp again. If your child hides behind your skirt when introduced to a stranger, you can bend down and wrap the skirt around her, saying proudly, "And this is Rebecca, in here somewhere." She'll laugh while you paw at her to try to "find" her. You and your child will figure out lots of ingenious ways to help her giggle away her fears. These activities will also keep you from the boredom of a staid and proper life.

One set of fears almost all children acquire involves name-calling. Once a child has been called a name in a scornful tone, the experience stays with her, annoying her like a pebble in her shoe. She doesn't understand it. Why would anyone target her? What did they mean? Her way of trying to get help with it is to play the same hurt out at others, which usually gets her in trouble with Mom or Dad. You can use playlistening to counsel her.

If your child is calling her sister "doo-doo head," you can playfully scurry into the room and, with warmth and affection, pummel her chest, saying, "Oooooh! I heard you say that awful thing! That was a *terrible* thing to call your sister!" Keep your voice high and light, so she knows you aren't at all angry. If she wants to work on name-calling, she'll say something like, "You're a doo-doo head, too!" You can bounce up and down and yelp, "I am *not* a doo-doo head! Oooooh, I'm going to get you now!" and move in for more pretend pummelling, which is actually a vigorous cuddle. The warmth and physical contact help your child feel safe enough to laugh and work through the hurt she felt when others rejected her. She was probably too stunned to defend herself at the time. Your exaggerated protest now makes her laugh very hard. This laughter will reduce her urge to earnestly act out what was done to her. It will also keep her from taking future insults so thoroughly to heart. Playing the affectionately insulted one works well to address other aggressive behaviors children acquire, too. A child can't retain her urge to hurt for long if you're playful and hunting for her giggles.

PLAYLISTENING PROVIDES ACCESS
TO DEEPER DISCHARGE

When a child has secured much laughter, she feels quite safe and loved. At this point, she will often spontaneously find a way to bring up deeper distresses she carries. She will become upset, sad, or frustrated, usually about something insignificant. For instance, she'll want her *red* sweater, which is in the wash, or she'll need a pencil with the *right* kind of eraser. She feels safe enough now to trust you with those upsets that stand in her way of feeling entirely good about her life. Wanting the *red* sweater or the *right* eraser lights a handy fuse which will soon ignite an old powder keg of feelings that don't make sense, but won't go away.

If you can stay close and supportive as the upset develops, not trying to placate her feelings or to "talk sense into her," she'll take the opportunity to tantrum or cry vigorously. These are the times that try parents' souls. All this emotion lit by what seems to be a totally insignificant issue! But this outburst is a blessing in disguise. When she is finished she'll have blasted away a heavy burden. She'll feel relaxed, refreshed, and much closer to you than before. These long hearty cries enable a child to release the distresses that keep her afraid and inflexible in her approach to life. Playlistening won't always result in ready access to deeper upsets. But when it does, remember that this, too, is part of the healing process you have initiated with humor and laughter.

MORE ABOUT SETTING LIMITS

After children have laughed away some of their lighter fears in active play, they sometimes ask for help with heavier fears they may carry. A child is asking for help with fear when, in the midst of wrestling and laughter, she intentionally elbows you hard in the ribs or pinches your arm with a mean grimace. Your child's mood has tightened, and she is suddenly out to hurt you or to damage something. It's time to set reasonable limits. Let her know, in a matter-of-fact tone, that you won't let her hurt you or do damage. "Sylvie, I won't let you scratch me." "Oops, Tanya! I can't let you bang on the window with your foot." Your limit-setting can be mildly stated and totally effective at the same time, as long as *you* take responsibility for physically stopping the behavior that goes overboard. *You* shield yourself from her scratching hands. *You* hold her kicking foot away from the window.

When a child's behavior goes beyond the boundaries of good sense, we usually expect her to listen to what we say and obey. She will almost never meet this expectation. She can't. She is no longer thinking. She is showing us troubles she hopes we can fix. She wants help badly, so she keeps on trying to pinch or to kick the window, showing how mean she feels. If you tell her what you won't allow and then take gentle but firm responsibility for seeing that the limit is kept, she will often be able to let the underlying tensions bubble up to be discharged in laughter, tears, or the sweaty struggling that expels fear.

For instance, father and son have been wrestling and laughing, in good communication, for a long while. Suddenly, son kicks father hard. Father says, "Whooah! That was too much! I don't think I want any more of those!" in a friendly, level voice. Son tries again, and father catches his foot in mid-air. Son laughs a lot as he struggles to get his foot away. Father lets him go at last, and they tussle with laughter. After a minute or two, son turns serious, tries to kick again, and father captures his foot between his legs. Son's mood is tightening. He is becoming more determined to hurt father. Some feelings of anger and alienation are coming to the fore. Soon, son can't laugh any more. His angry feelings have engulfed him. Father stays close, as gentle as he can be while protecting himself. Son tries repeatedly to kick, but Father won't let go of his feet. If he did, he would get hurt. Father says, "I can't let you hurt me. If I let go, you're going to kick me hard, so I think I'd better hold onto your feet for now. I won't hurt you, son." If father is kind enough as he reaches for his angry son, his child will begin to cry hard, tremble, and perspire. He'll have the safety he needs to discharge this upset that makes him feel mean and hurtful.

There is much more to be said about handling our children's deeper fears. If your child brings up hurtful behavior in the midst of play, it will help you to read the chapters "Healing Children's Fears," "Crying," and "Reaching For Your Angry Child." The important point here is that playlistening may lead your child to request help with distresses that cause hurtful behavior. You will need to set limits when this happens. Your choices are basically to stay with your child as she discharges her heavier upset or to stop playlistening as soon as "overboard" behavior starts, and get out the baseball mitts, the milk and sandwiches, or the color crayons. If you choose to sidestep your child's request for help because you are not yet ready to handle her fears, rest assured that she won't give up. Children are very persistent in their attempts to get help with their deeper distresses.

CHALLENGES AND REWARDS

Playlistening is good for us, too. To do it we have to train ourselves to bounce a little, clown a little. In play, we have a good antidote to the worries and cares that can sour adult life. Children are experts at relieving their tensions through laughter. If you follow your child's lead, you'll have a master teacher who will be delighted to help you remember to laugh and play.

Most parents can learn this counseling skill more easily with the help of regular Co-Counseling sessions and parent support groups. These opportunities to connect with other parents and to focus on our relationships with our children can help change parenting from an endurance feat to the rewarding endeavor we hoped it would be.

CRYING

WHEN YOUR CHILD BEGINS TO CRY

In listening to parents over the years, I have learned a simple truth: parents want good lives for their children. We want our children to be happy, loved, respected, and understood. We also want the chance to correct the mistakes our parents made with us. For most of us, these goals are far more difficult to achieve than we had imagined. We discover that loving and nurturing a child is complex work that challenges the hardiest grownup. Help is scarce as we juggle too much work, too little time, and the constant call of our children to "Come and play, Daddy!" and, "Watch this, Mommy!"

It's no wonder, then, we become troubled when our children start to cry. To us, their crying often feels like parental failure. The scene is familiar: we are shuffling through the day in reasonably good spirits, balancing the children's needs, our needs, and that long mental list of things to be done. One of the children wants a cracker. When the box turns up empty he begins to cry. At this moment, our insides curdle. We become annoyed, worried, tired, exasperated. We try to stop him from crying. Our tactics might be to soothe him, to try to talk him into a cracker substitute, to point out his mistake in wanting crackers before dinner, or to scold him when he doesn't stop crying over something so silly. We want the crying to stop so the hurt will go away.

If we watch closely, though, we may notice that the hurt doesn't always go away when the crying stops. A child may quiet down, but often he'll still feel upset. He will droop and refuse to look at anyone. Or he might become angry at the people he loves. An incident that begins with tears about a small thing, perhaps a broken truck or a torn homework paper, can turn into a long period of frustration and upset. The child can't seem to "come around" and trust other people again. He isn't satisfied, the parents are peeved, and family life doesn't flow smoothly.

As Co-Counselors, we are fortunate to have access to a different approach to crying. If we listen and stay close, without interrupting his tears, a child will cry until his upset resolves. Here is the headline: Crying Heals the Hurt. And because you have let your child be in charge of discharging his hurt feelings, he will come away stronger and surer of himself. Listening is a powerful tool that can transform children's upsets into opportunities for them to gain confidence. Listening lets you work *with* your child. He does the work of eliminating his bad feelings, and you stay close, offering the support he needs to emerge full of trust and hope when he's finished. We get to play a powerful, healing role when we stop and listen to a child who begins to cry.

CRYING IS A NATURAL RECOVERY PROCESS

One way to understand our children's need to cry is to picture them perched on a narrow balance beam of confidence. On this beam, their sunny optimism allows them to learn quickly and to trust us when we offer suggestions or help. They feel secure and loved, and they experiment constantly. When their experiments don't work, they simply try again. (Remember how many falls your toddler took as he learned to walk?) But this precious sense of confidence and closeness is easily disrupted. When their best efforts fail too often, or when the people around them seem remote or disapproving, children's feelings are hurt, and they fall from this narrow beam on which the world feels safe and good. Thrown "off track," our children can't find the confidence they need to keep trying. They feel sad and begin to cry.

The approach of listening to a child at times like these is based on the insight that crying is part of a recovery process. Your child cries in order to shed his hurt feelings. As you stay with him, he gathers a sense of being supported and cared about at the very same time that he feels his worst. From his point of view, his life is falling apart, and there you are by his side, riding out the storm with him. Once your child has discharged by crying, he returns to his life refreshed. His confidence, hope, and intelligence shift into gear, allowing him to learn and love well again. When you listen as your child cries, you enable him to learn as he faces tough challenges and to recover from the incidents that hurt him.

SMALL INCIDENTS GIVE RISE TO BIG FEELINGS

This recovery process—crying until the hurt is gone—comes naturally to our children. They try to use it whenever they are having trouble feeling loved and confident. When a child lacks the confidence to make it through the next half hour, he'll usually choose a very small issue as the focus of his upset. For instance, after being excluded from play by his sister all afternoon, your younger child asks for a piece of toast. You serve him one, and he bursts into sobs. You cut it into triangles: he wanted rectangles! If you simply kneel down, put your arm around him and listen, the crying can go on for a long time. The triangular toast feels tragic to him: it's the last straw after hearing "I don't want you around! Go away!" all afternoon. Your child is not petty or manipulative. This is the way all children (not just infants and toddlers) ask for help at the low moments in their lives. We adults are not that different. Often, for instance, when we feel most alone, we don't begin to cry about it until we stub our toe on the doorjamb or until the toilet overflows. These are the kinds of little incidents that open the door to far bigger feelings.

The little issues that allow your child to cry can irritate you greatly unless you remember that they often stand for bigger issues. There will be times, at the end of a long cry about a piece of toast cut the wrong way or a broken cookie, when your child will be able to tell you what the real issue was: "Mommy, I saw a show on TV when you were out, and in it the mother got sick and died," or, "Daddy, I want you to love me as much as you love Rachel." Other times, your child will cry, then finish and romp off to play without saying anything. We parents desperately want to know what causes our children such grief, but there are *many* times when they have no words for how they feel. Fortunately, it is enough that we listen. With us by their sides, they can get the important recovery work done, even when we don't understand exactly what that work is.

HAPPY TIMES OFTEN BRING UP UNFINISHED GRIEFS

As if to make parenting even more of a test of character, children often choose happy, close times with you to bring up feelings of upset. I call this the "spoiled outing" phenomenon. You have just spent a happy day with your children, perhaps at the park or with their cousins, playing and doing the things they love. As you head for home, your children become unhappy and easily upset. They cry about having to sit in the back seat, over your request that each child carry his own jacket, or because you've stopped at McDonalds, not Burger King. A parent's mood at moments like these tends to be grim: "If this is how you act, I'm not bringing you to the park again!"

What the children are actually doing is taking advantage of the extra feelings of safety and closeness they have gathered throughout the day. The backdrop of a day's satisfaction makes the imperfections in life stand out like spaghetti stains on a white tablecloth. Because he's had such a happy day, your child now turns to address sadness he still carries. For your child, it's an efficient way to flush out stored upsets. If you don't expect it, however, a "spoiled outing" can be frustrating or even infuriating. Once you realize that it happens like clockwork, you are in a much better position to listen as your child cries his upsets into peace of mind. For instance, you can begin to head for home before all your energy is spent, knowing that along the way there will be some constructive falling apart to be done.

GUIDELINES FOR THE LISTENER

The following are basic steps to take as your child makes use of this deeply effective discharge process.

- **Remedy any physically harmful situation, and remove any real danger from the scene.**

This means pulling pinched fingers out of toys, lifting your child's fallen bike from off his leg, or holding off siblings or playmates who might be upset enough to hurt him. Do the sensible thing, as calmly as you can.

- **Keep your own upset and advice to yourself.**

Your child is looking for your support now that you have arrived and are listening. Adding your own upset or advice will only complicate his efforts to understand what has happened to him. For instance, if your child fell while running, simply listen and hold him. You'll be tempted to scold him or lecture him about the wet pavement. Don't give in to this impulse. As he cries, your child blocks most of his surroundings out of his mind, focusing entirely on how he feels and on your reassuring presence. He has narrowed his focus to do the work of recovery. He can't complete this task without concentrating on it fully. Don't distract him with a lecture on how he could have done things better. While he is crying, he can't process the advice you give, and any anger you might express only adds to his hurt. Your role is that of counselor, not critic.

After he has cried fully and is feeling safe and sure of himself again, he'll be eager to learn from what happened with just a touch of help from you. "See where you slipped? It's wet there," is all you'll need to say. Because his crying has cleared away the confusion he felt, he can respond proudly, "Oh, I slipped on the wet part. I'm going to run slow where it's wet, Daddy. Watch me!"

- **Move close to your child, holding him gently so he can make eye contact with you.**

Touch and loving eye contact are two of the most powerful reassurances we can give. Hold your child so that he can see you if he chooses. Don't put him over your shoulder to cry or let him stay buried in your lap for long. Your gentle encouragement to take a look at you will remind your child of your love. If he sees your loving gaze, he will most likely cry harder because he sees how much you care. However, he may not be able to look at you at all. Don't worry. It simply means that he is concentrating on sad feelings and isn't finished discharging yet. After more crying and your patient encouragement he will be able to relax and make full contact with you again.

When your child is in tears, all his defenses are down. As he focuses on his sadness, your response makes a deep impression. Your tender touch, your caress on his cheek, the way you cradle him in your arms, a gentle kiss now and then on his fingers bring your caring straight to your child's heart. Few words from you are needed. Your child will probably not acknowledge your affection, but when you see how fully he relaxes afterwards you'll know that he absorbed every bit of your love.

- **Gently invite him to tell you what the trouble is. Do not insist on any particular response.**

Children who have begun to cry always have a reason, a good reason, for their feelings. The deeper the feelings, the harder it is for the child to talk about them. Tell him that you want to understand what happened; then simply accept whatever he can tell or show you. At times, the mere thought of talking about troubles will keep a child's tears flowing long before any words can be spoken. You will not be totally in the dark about how he feels, however. The tone of his cry, the look on his face, how he looks at you (or shuts his eyes tight) can tell you a great deal about this upset. Stay keenly tuned to him, whether he can talk about his troubles or not.

One child I know often had a hard time when one of her parents was gone on a business trip. Once, when her father was out of town, two-year-old Amy was especially upset when her mother left her at day care. In the evening, her caregiver reported that she had been sad, withdrawn, and touchy most of the day. That night when Amy and her mother got home, Amy was dissatisfied with everything her mother did. The mother went to Amy, put her arms around her, and said, "Let's talk about what's so hard." Amy cried and screamed for a long time in her mother's arms. She said nothing but was obviously working through a great upset. Her mother, guessing that she was missing her father, periodically reassured her that her dad was coming back. When Amy stopped crying she didn't seem quite at peace, so her mother asked, "Amy, what is it that has you so worried?" Amy, who had said nothing during her long cry, looked at her mother and said emphatically, "The kitten we gave to Grandma had a mother, but *it's* mother isn't coming back!" Two weeks before, they had picked a kitten out of a litter and brought it to Grandma. It was now easy to see how her father's absence had triggered so much grief— she was thinking, "If this is what we do to kitties, what will happen to me?" Informed at last, her mother could explain that mothers, fathers, and children stay close all their lives, and cats and kittens don't. Amy seemed satisfied, closed her eyes, and slept for fourteen hours. Her next day was much more relaxed. Amy shed her griefs first and talked about them later, when she could digest the information she needed. Crying first, talking second, then new understandings—this is often how it goes.

- **If you see that your child is afraid of something specific, reassure him that you'll protect him from that particular danger.**

Your reassurances serve as a gentle reminder of reality for a child who is awash with feelings. For example, "Mommy will come back after shopping. She will *always* come back to you." "Randy didn't mean to break your glider. He's sorry, too." "Your knee will heal up soon. The hurting won't last much longer." Don't expect your child to stop crying just because you say it's safe. Do give the reassurances you think he might need as he works toward his own sense of safety.

- **Don't pass judgment on what your child feels.**

This is hard to do! We are so accustomed to seeing the world only from our own vantage point. If we don't feel sad, no one else should, either. Children's feelings are like their own personal weather system, which is affected by forces often unseen by you. To tell your child he should feel happy when he is sad is roughly as effective as telling a rainstorm to go away. Phrases like "I'm sorry you feel so sad," or, "I'll stay right here with you while it's hard," give your child permission to address and discharge bad feelings. Phrases like "Don't feel sorry for yourself, you started this fight!" and "It's only a torn paper. Quit acting like such a baby!" only shame a child. Such statements work against your goal of helping your child rebuild his sense of well-being.

As you listen, you are not necessarily condoning your child's feelings, nor are you spoiling him. You are helping him recover. Children cry only when they are too upset to think. Feelings of upset can overpower a child and drive him to do things that don't make sense, which is exactly why your child is trying to cry them away. He hates to be "off track," out of control of his life. As you listen, you drain the power these feelings have over your child. His own good judgment will return once you've listened thoroughly.

As your child cries, you may hear strong complaints about you or about other important people in your child's life. "You don't love me, and you never did!" "I wish you weren't my mommy." "I hate you, Dad! Everybody else's dad is better than you." "I hate my brother. I want to kill him! He stinks, and I never want to see him again!" These are the kinds of things that children say while they are discharging distress. To cry away the hurt and regain their good nature, children need what one friend of mine calls "freedom of the mouth." If they can cry and tell you the worst of how they feel, their bitterness will drain away. (It helps to let a child know, "However you feel, I'll always love you.") Don't take these feelings too person-ally. What a child says as he is crying isn't his lifetime evaluation of you. It represents only the hurt he's busy flushing out. He'll be back in touch with how good you are just as soon as he's rid of these prickly feelings.

- **Allow plenty of time for your child to cry.**

Your child will cry first about the incident that just happened and may then go on to cry about other important things without telling you that he has switched topics. If listening is a new approach in your family, his cries may at first be long and hearty; half an hour or an hour would not be unusual. He has been waiting for this opportunity for quite awhile. The warmer and kinder you are, the longer and more intensely he will cry because he is relieved to feel your support and caring. Many of us remember having tears come to our eyes when someone was unexpectedly kind to us at a time of crisis. For your child, it's just like that. The safer things are, the more fully he can show you his feelings and the deeper his sense of relief and well-being will be after his cry is over.

At the mention of time, we parents throw up our hands in frustration. Where are we supposed to come by these half-hours to sit and listen to one of our children? Who will make the dinner? Who will referee the squabbles the other children are bound to have? Time is a precious commodity in the lives of parents, and most of us bridle at the thought of spending more time or trying harder.

There is no easy answer to the problem of lack of time. However, many parents find that when you treat crying as a recovery process, you are relieved of certain unpleasant duties. Scolding, worrying, and endlessly trying to placate your child when he is irritable are unnecessary. Now, when nothing satisfies your cranky child, you can simply sit down with him in your arms for a few moments and allow him to cry to his heart's content, knowing that it's his turn to work through his sadness and your turn to relax, listen, and let your love seep back into his heart.

• **Sleep may follow a child's extended cry.**

There are a couple of ways sleep may play a part in this recovery process. At the end of a hearty cry, a child may yawn a few times, nestle into your arms, and fall quickly into a deep sleep. This sleep is important. It gives a child the time and peace to assemble a more rational perspective than his feelings of hurt have allowed. He will most often awaken relaxed and ready to enjoy his life.

Alternatively, sleep will sometimes serve as an intermission rather than as the completion of the recovery process. In the middle of a set of deep, unhappy feelings, a child may head raggedly toward sleep, with continued crying now and then as he drops off. He awakens feeling miserable, with renewed energy to finish tangling with the sizeable chunk of upset he has challenged. When crying involves a child fully enough that sleep is this kind of intermission, you are likely to see significant positive changes in his behavior. He is lifting an especially heavy load from his mind and heart.

• **Look for new and more flexible play, insights, warmth, and creativity from your child after you've listened through a full cry.**

Children feel relaxed, well-loved, and hopeful after a good cry with adult support. In small but significant ways, they let us know that they see things differently now. A child might tenderly brush back the hair from your face after bitter tears and words, venture to play with children he was afraid of, make up little songs of happiness, or finish the math homework he couldn't face before. Keep your eye out for glimpses of his genius for living and loving. You don't want to miss the fuller affection he'll feel toward you, or the signs of his growing confidence. These are the rewards of good listening. You've earned them!

One mother I know was having a heartwrenching time leaving her daughter at nursery school. The child would cling, complain, and cry every morning as the mother left, stop crying soon after, then spend her days shy and withdrawn. Finally, the mother decided to come to school early, begin saying goodbye, and stay with her daughter while she cried the hurt through. For each of the first three mornings, the mother listened to about an hour of deeply-felt grief in their car. When her daughter stopped crying, she would gently say, "It's time to go in to school. Are you ready to go with me?" and her daughter would sob and cling some more. Each morning, after what seemed to be an impossibly long cry, the daughter would finally stop, look around a bit, peek in her lunchbox or play with the steering wheel, and then agree to go to school. The fourth morning, the daughter cried harder than ever for fifteen minutes, then rather quickly decided she wanted to go in. The fifth morning, there were no tears. Daughter gave her mother a big, long hug and said she wanted to go up the walkway to the school by herself. Her mother followed a moment later to sign her in and saw that her daughter had put her things away and was already at play. The caregivers reported a marked change in the daughter's confidence during the course of that week, a change which was finally evident to the mother on that fifth day.

Another example: One twenty-two-month-old boy had an eye infection which was to be treated with eye drops. As his mother told him about the medicine and how she was going to put it in his eye, he began to cry very hard. Curious about what would happen if she listened and didn't force this issue, she held the bottle so he could see it, cuddled up to him, and listened while he cried. He began to slow down after about forty-five minutes, so she asked him if he wanted her to open the bottle so he could see the dropper. He cried another ten minutes about that idea. When she asked again, he said yes. She opened the bottle and demonstrated how the drops would come out. More hard crying. She told him she had to put the drops in, but that he could try the dropper out first if he wanted. He touched it, then threw himself back to cry again. After some time, he got up and started to squeeze the medicine out of the dropper carefully into the bottle. His mother let him practice awhile and then reminded him that they had to get this medicine into his eyes. He cried again, but for a short time only. Then he asked if he could do it himself. She told him he could try. He lay back, she put the proper amount of medicine into the dropper, and he unblinkingly squeezed two drops into each eye, with only one misplaced splash on his nose. She was amazed. Thereafter, he was utterly calm about eyedrops and often chose to put them in himself.

Children who, like the young ones above, are given support to cry fully about the challenges which face them are eventually able to develop surprising confidence in their own abilities. It may require a series of many "sessions," during which your child feels utterly helpless, in order to clear away a hurt. But the child you see after each cry will feel and act less helpless than before.

LISTENING TO CHILDREN ISN'T EASY FOR PARENTS

Listening to a crying child is a simple act, quite beneficial to the child, but it's not easy. To be fully present with our children while they recover from their upsets, we parents need time to discharge our feelings, too. Our children's strong emotions stir up our own. We have lots to talk about: how difficult it is to be parents, how much we love our children, the things they do that irritate us, our worries, our disappointments, our hopes for them.

This is where regular Co-Counseling sessions are invaluable. As we discharge on our childhood distresses, we become better listeners, more confident that a good cry is a gift to a child. As we let a listener know how sad and tired we get, we shed the patterns of worry, impatience, and disapproval our parents unwittingly passed on to us. We break the cycle of oppression that cramps young people's lives and regain more of our own good-natured intelligence in the process.

TANTRUMS AND INDIGNATION

A NEW SET OF ASSUMPTIONS

Most of us who are parents measure our competence in a very straightforward way. When our children are happy, cooperative, loving, and polite, we are able to take pride in our parenting and in them. When our children are unhappy or unreasonable, we either blame ourselves or we blame our children. Most of the world operates on the assumption that children's upsets are "bad." With heavy persuasion or force, we have been trained to pressure our children to be quiet and "good" again because we don't want to feel like "bad" parents with "bad" children.

There is a fresh approach, however, that relieves mothers and fathers of the unpleasant and difficult job of trying to make children be "good." It is based on Re-evaluation Counseling, which makes these generous but well-founded assumptions:

- **Children are naturally easy-going, loving, cooperative, and eager to learn.**

- **Children's good nature can be obscured by bad feelings.**

  When children are sad, frightened, frustrated, embarrassed, or when they feel alone or unappreciated, their

43

good nature can be obscured. Such tensions pull a child's behavior "off track," away from trust, cooperation, and enthusiasm.

- **Hurt feelings confine a child to unloving, fearful, or inflexible behavior, which is a clear request for help.**

- **A child who is upset or inflexible will recover from his feelings of hurt if a caring adult moves in warmly and listens while he discharges his upset.**

Parents who adopt this new approach to troublesome times soon find that a child's upset, which once seemed to indicate a serious failure, now simply signals the need for some discharge. A parent's gentle attention encourages the child to feel the upset fully. With great energy, he will cry, tantrum, tremble, or laugh until he has shed the feelings that drove his judgment off course. Children's emotional outbursts are a natural recovery process that restores their ability to relax, love, and learn. We have found that children whose deep feelings are listened to, develop confidence in their own strength and intelligence, and confidence in their parents' love. Hope and affection spring into a child's heart after his noisy, vigorously unhappy feelings have been shed.

In particular, frustration is a common trouble that besets anyone who is eagerly learning new skills. Children approach learning with an "Of course I can do it!" attitude and a real passion for success. Their ideas of what they want to do are grand, yet children's abilities grow only through the messy process of trial and error. Feelings of frustration are an everyday glitch in the learning process, a natural result of the clash between what children expect and what they are able to do.

FRUSTRATION CLOGS THE LEARNING PROCESS

Frustration is a perplexing foe of learners of all ages. We all know how it builds: a child can't make things go his way, and to his credit, he won't give up trying. Eventually he loses his ability to come up with new approaches. He wants to succeed but can't figure out how. He feels like jumping out of his skin. Suggestions from a well-meaning adult won't help because his feelings have overwhelmed his ability to think. At this point, if tantrums are forbidden, the child must abandon his attempt to learn. Frustration will bristle like a porcupine every time he faces similar situations or similar learning tasks.

HOW CHILDREN RECOVER FROM FRUSTRATION

When a frustrated child feels safe, he begins a tantrum, the discharge process that expels frustration. Bursting into lots of noise and motion, his body becomes hot, and there may be tears and perspiration as well. A child will often throw himself to the ground, arms and legs flying, or push himself against an immovable object and keep pushing to no avail. Tantrums are not usually directed at anyone in particular. They are not mean-spirited or spiteful. The child's outburst is a lively release of tension that ignites in an instant.

Tantrums aren't a pretty sight to most parents, but you will come to appreciate them when you see how deeply they relieve your child. Most of us have never seen a tantrum restore a child's ability to think and learn because we are surrounded by people who become angry or threatening when children show their feelings. We've been taught that children are not supposed to have tantrums, although every healthy child tries again and again to relieve frustration in this way.

A tantrum doesn't necessarily mean that anything is wrong with you, the situation, or your child. Repeated tantrums in similar situations, though, might mean that inappropriate expectations or limitations are being placed on your child's behavior. For instance, expecting a young child to do a round of shopping without touching anything is bound to result in frustration. Young children can't quell their instinctive desire to learn, and they learn by touching. Even when our expectations fit our children well, they are bound to become frustrated at times. Their hopes and ideas outreach their abilities. Tantrums are the way children face that frustration, get rid of it, and return to a satisfying life.

When we allow a child's tantrum to run its full course, he is freed from the tension that clogs his learning process. A frustrated child makes the same mistakes over and over. He cannot accept help from anyone. After a healthy tantrum a child relaxes with what he can do and returns to the joys of learning and cooperation. Tantrums play an important role in keeping children hopeful about their intelligence. Given this outlet, they don't have to walk away from challenges whenever the learning process becomes difficult.

LISTENING TO YOUR CHILD'S TANTRUMS

You probably can think of several situations that regularly frustrate your child. Sometimes it's an event that triggers the upset, such as being strapped into the car seat, having little brother barge in on a game, or being asked to draw something for school. Sometimes tantrums seem to be connected more to a time of day than to one particular kind of activity. For instance, coming home after day care or leaving home in the morning can be touchy times for children because they don't have much say in what happens at these times. After you've identified these times or activities, prepare yourself. Rather than hope that this persistent trouble has disappeared overnight, decide that it will probably erupt as usual. When your child becomes edgy, remember that he needs you to be his counselor, and move closer. If he is close to giving up on a frustrating effort, gently support him to stay where he is. Quietly, gently help him face how awful he feels.

Sometimes the beginning part of listening to a child's tantrum involves deciding not to placate your upset child. If your child has chosen one dress to wear for school but starts a tantrum when you try to put it on, you might ask her what other dress she wants. If she starts to fuss about the second dress she chose, you can be sure you have a child who is seeking the relief of a tantrum. All you need to do to help your child recover is to stop finding dresses. Gently say, "I think you'll have to choose one of these dresses you picked out." This gives her permission to begin.

Listening to your child's tantrums isn't much different from listening through a good cry, once you get the feel of it. (See the pamphlet *Crying*.) It's simply the thunder and lightning side of a child's internal weather system. Here are some general guidelines.

• **Stay close to your child but don't try to comfort him.**

A tantrum is full of noise and movement. Your child will become very hot and may perspire heavily. He needs to writhe, wiggle, and throw himself around to get the frustration out of his system. You can be safety manager, making sure that he doesn't bump into anything as he proceeds. All that stomping, noise, and struggle with unseen forces is helping him recover from the insult of not being able to make his own ideas work. (You know the feeling!) Let him move.

Most tantrums are relatively short. You might expect to listen for five to fifteen minutes. Once it is listened through, a tantrum clears rapidly, perhaps with some giggles and warm affection between child and listener. This transformation of your fallen-apart child into a gently reasonable person is one of the real wonders listening can produce. He will often gain a large store of patience that you'll appreciate during the following hours or days.

• **If you are in a public place, you may want to carefully carry your child to your car or other more sheltered spot to ride out the storm.**

Children often seem to pick public places to initiate tantrums. It may be that they feel safer to explode with lots of people around, or perhaps the strain of being in an adult environment finally overloads their tolerance for frustration.

Often it's worth the trouble to carry your writhing child to a less public spot so you feel freer to handle things thoughtfully. If you have no car nearby, the delivery side of the grocery store, the less popular underwear and socks section of the department store, or the front steps of your temple or church may have to serve as a makeshift refuge while your child works things through. Ask for help if you need it: "Would you move my grocery cart to one side? I'll be back in a few minutes." If you can manage it, a touch of humor helps: "Looks like we have technical difficulties! I do want to buy these sheets: I'll be back when my friend here feels better." Most onlookers will be glad that you look like you know what you're doing. In fact, most onlookers have at one time or another faced the same situation you are facing. Don't worry too much about them.

One parent I know, caught by a full tantrum in a crowded downtown toy store, had no good place to go;

so he walked the streets carrying his wriggling, yelping child for the ten-minute duration. His wife, embarrassed by the commotion, walked half a block behind them. When it was over, they expected their two year old to be tired and cranky, as was his usual habit early in the afternoon. They dared to enter a coffee shop for lunch, where their son charmed the waitress and sat, contented and alert, through a peaceful meal.

INDIGNATION

Another emotion our parents had little tolerance for is indignation. It's sometimes hard for us to distinguish between frustration and indignation because both are loud and both are beyond the boundaries of good manners and self-control that were drawn for most of us. Indignation is a spontaneous, healthy response to injustice. It is one of those culturally forbidden expressions which, when understood and listened through, will serve both your child and your family well.

Sometimes our children have good reason to be indignant about the treatment they receive from us, other adults, and their peers. Disrespect for young people is widespread in our society. When confident young people are wronged, they will heatedly protest. Their response is immediate, fresh, loud, and not aimed to hurt anyone. They aim to be heard and to set things right. An indignant child will tell you (or someone else) in no uncertain terms what he thinks was thoughtless or unfair. "Don't you talk to my brother like that! You're being mean to him. Just be quiet!" "You can't call me stupid just because I lost my homework! I am not stupid! Never say that again!" "You think that all kids who have punk haircuts are delinquents! You are so wrong! I want you to stop insulting my friends! I can't stand it anymore!" These are examples of how a young person will stand up for what he thinks is right. Infants and toddlers will also insist on respectful treatment, without words but with complete seriousness of purpose. People seem to be born with an innate expectation of love and respect. Only illness or repeated mistreatment wears down a person's will to fight for what's right.

When we parents are one step ahead of the exhaustion of raising children, it can be a relief to have our children stop us short when we are being harsh or unfair. Ultimately we want our children to retain their keen sense of justice and to insist on the respect they deserve, even if it's our behavior they challenge. They do well to defend themselves against our tired, irrational, troubled words and actions.

LISTENING TO INDIGNATION

When a child thinks that he or someone he cares about has been wronged and he becomes indignant, our best move is to hear him out. What is he saying? Is he right? What can be done about it? When an indignant person meets with good listening and genuine remedies, the incident is soon over and the upset is resolved. An apology, a change of decision, or a promise of a full discussion about the issue are the kinds of remedies we can offer. If you listen and then work with your child to make things right, he'll be satisfied and pleased with himself and with you.

For example, when my two sons would get into their inevitable arguments, I sometimes would listen and become convinced that one son was at fault. I would angrily enter into the fray, blaming one and defending the other. Many times, the son I was defending would turn to me and yell, "Get out of here, Mom! You're blaming him, and you don't know anything about this! You gang up on him and make it worse. This is our fight!" I would stomp away insulted, of course, and surprised. They would go back to their fight, mad at each other again, but without my upset to deal with. Were they "nice" to me? No, they were righteous. Did they defend themselves for good reason? Yes. They were fighting for a solution, and my blame was adding to the problem. Do they yell at me every time I say something in the midst of a fight? No. If I'm sensible and I ask pertinent questions rather than assign blame, they will often use my help. Our children's indignation can keep us from sloppiness in our treatment of them and others. Their finely tuned sense of justice can be a real gift in our lives.

IS THIS LISTENING APPROACH TOO PERMISSIVE?

If I listen to tantrums and indignation, will my child ever be well-behaved again? This is *the* question. It feels like there are too many times when messy upsets arise. If we listen every time, won't life become an uproar? Aren't we reinforcing lack of control? How will we stand this behavior?

Allowing a child's tantrums to run their course or allowing indignation to be heard may indeed be hair-raising for a parent the first few times. It can feed our fears of chaos, and it often angers us to see such raw feelings. We take a child's feelings personally, as if our child is giving us a failing grade in parenting. Our interpretations of tantrums and indignation are strong and negative, and we do need Co-Counseling sessions—regular and full of discharge—to contend with what goes on inside of us.

The theory we have available to us as RCers is elegant and simple, but as parents we don't have an easy time applying it. We need close, loving counseling relationships in which we can confess and discharge our own feelings about having a frustrated or indignant child. Given the chance to focus on the situations that gnaw at our patience, we can wade into the thick of the action with cooler heads and a more intentional approach.

Many parents who first begin to listen to their children's tantrums and indignation find their children eager to release these tensions. You may be treated to several lively outbursts a day at first if your child has been on edge. But as his backlog of frustrated feelings drains, you'll see a much happier and sturdier child emerge. He'll certainly run into new situations that frustrate him, because he is an eager learner. But once the backlog is listened through, he won't bristle with tension in every challenging situation. Children love to be in good contact with others. They love to be sure enough of themselves to move without upset from one adventure to another. They have tantrums only when they need to heal from an adventure that overwhelmed their confidence.

One mother I know was lamenting her son's entrance into the "terrible twos." He had been feisty and stubborn for a week or two, wanting each detail of life to be just so, with no adult interference. When she moved in close and listened, he had several tantrums over a three- or four-day period and then returned to his usual easygoing ways. His "personality change" had simply been the need to get a few things off his chest before he could re-establish his pleasure in himself and others.

Children don't pick easy times and places for their tantrums or indignation, so don't expect that your good listening will result in a perfectly polite child. While he is young, your child will tantrum when he needs to. The children whose parents have listened to them in this way have not gone into adolescence falling apart with every little frustration. They have taken advantage of this outlet during childhood and have gathered lots of flexibility and confidence in the process.

Using this approach, you can expect that your child will become increasingly able to meet important challenges. He'll persist in learning even when he has difficulties, and he'll defend his integrity in the face of irrationality. These strengths will stand him in far better stead throughout his life than strict adherence to the rules of etiquette. Relieved of tension, he'll be able to be genuinely pleased with people most of the time. Listened to when he's upset, he'll learn real empathy because that's how you've treated him.

HEALING CHILDREN'S FEARS

WHERE DO CHILDREN'S FEARS COME FROM?

Children are born into the world knowing very little, and they arrive expecting love, gentleness, and understanding. While parents provide as much love and attention as they can, one or two adults aren't always enough to provide all the attention and tenderness a young child expects. When things happen that children don't comprehend, or when they are left alone too much, they can easily become frightened. Many experiences which seem harmless and matter-of-fact to grown-ups can frighten a child, who is keenly tuned to sense tensions we take for granted. In particular, our children are unprepared for sudden, painful, or thoughtless occurrences. Early separation from mother or father; sudden, unexplained changes in who cares for her; tense conversations within the family; teasing by aggressive relatives; or exposure to violence on TV are the kinds of things that can frighten a child, even though nothing physically harmful has happened.

In addition, some children face direct physical trauma very early in life. A long or difficult birth, prematurity, treatment for jaundice, even circumcision, can frighten an infant and diminish the blessings of peace and ease during the first months of life. Some children, because of serious trauma, lead lives which are always tense with underlying fear.

When a child feels frightened, she has difficulty staying in close contact with her loved ones. She can't hold your gaze for long, and will either be slow to experiment and to trust people, or will be constantly "on the go," unable to slow down and enjoy your presence in a relaxed way. Fear also makes children edgy and hard to please: things have to be "just so" or the frightened child flares with impatience or anger. Life does not roll easily from one sunny pastime to the next for the young child who is afraid.

Sometimes, you'll be called upon to help your child recover from her fears just after the fright has occurred. For example, a bounding dog has just been pulled away from your child, who is standing unhurt, but terrified and screaming. More frequently, your child will come to you with a fear she has had for some time. Nothing real threatens her, but fear grips her just the same. The child who was once frightened by a bounding dog is seized by that same fear when invited to touch a dozing classroom rabbit. A child who has always been afraid of meeting new people is panicked again on the first day of first grade.

HOW CHILDREN RECOVER FROM THEIR FEARS

We parents can help our children recover completely from their fears. Few of us have seen more than a moment or two of the the recovery process our children try to use. It is a difficult one for parents to support, because when children are discharging fear, they feel deeply afraid. Children discharge their fears as they tremble, cry loudly with or without tears, perspire, and have active kidneys. Children need us to come close and listen through their fears, just as they need us to come close and listen when they cry. While children recover from grief they feel utterly sad, as though the heartbreak will never end. Similarly, as you move closer to your fearful child, her fears will become more intense. She may struggle against you as she trembles and perspires. Messy and noisy though it may be, this process is very efficient. Over time, a fussy, timid, or belligerent child will transform her whole demeanor and approach to life if given the chance to discharge the fears she carries. By listening to panic and frantic fear, you can clear important stumbling blocks from your child's life. You can help her reclaim the confidence her fears have pirated away.

Your child has probably made repeated attempts to use the discharge process to shed her fears. Frightened infants will try to recover by screaming loudly with their eyes shut tight and their little chins trembling. They move vigorously, and perspire and tremble as they scream, often pushing with their legs or pulling at their ears. After infancy, children screech and run to cling to an adult they trust the moment something frightens them. If allowed, they will tremble, struggle, perspire, and scream as the adult holds them close and patiently asks what happened.

Seeing a child feel fear during this recovery process is disturbing for most parents: the healing process frightens us, so we do everything in our power to stop it. We have been taught to soothe, distract, or scold. We stop the healing process because we equate stopping the child from showing her fear with eliminating the fear. Nothing could be farther from the truth. The child stops, and retains her fear. If she can't finish crying and trembling the fear away, she can't emerge to face what she was so afraid of and understand that she survived. Her behavior will be governed by that unresolved fear at times which do not always seem to relate to the fearful incident. She might wake up repeatedly with nightmares, or avoid certain activities that scare her. When one of my sons became afraid to part with me at the age of thirteen months, he stopped walking with me to the park. He insisted on being carried. If I put him down and asked him to walk, he would scream, perspire, and dive for my arms in fear. I didn't understand at the time that he needed to feel the fear and expel it so he could get on with his quest for independence. Children's attempts to work on fear are very confusing: who would guess that letting them be overcome with fear in your arms could cut a straight path toward confidence?

CHILDREN OFTEN SHOW THEIR FEARS INDIRECTLY

Sometimes, children can't initiate the discharge process in a straightforward way. They can't scream and run for help because they have become afraid to feel afraid. Instead, they ask for help by pointedly "going overboard." Either they insist on avoiding certain activities, people, or places, or they act aggressively in situations that frighten them. It is also common for children's fears to surface indirectly in the form of anger. (See "Reaching For Your Angry Child.")

The following are a few guidelines for counseling a child on fear. They will give you the basic information you need once your child has cried out in her fear and you have arrived to help. Information on how you can assist children who are showing fears indirectly, through avoidance or aggression, will follow, after the basic guidelines for being counselor are outlined here.

- **Hold your child close, and be sure that she can see you fully when she chooses.**

A terrified child needs you close. She needs to feel your body right next to hers, and she needs to see your calm, caring face whenever she opens her eyes. She is re-living a frightening time, and when she looks out at you, she is checking to make sure that you aren't swept away by her fear, too. Do what you can to show confidence that all is well. She needs you to provide steady contradiction to the panic she is trying to expel. While working through fear, a child you are holding in your arms will sometimes scream and arch her back, throwing her head back with her eyes shut tight. Gently but persistently draw her toward you again and encourage her to look at you. Tell her that you will stay close, and that she can see you anytime she is ready.

- **Stay close, even if your child struggles to fight you off.**

Your child's fear must have a focus in order for the discharge process to work. You will usually be the safest, most reliable focus around. So as you move close to try to help, your child may begin to push you away, transferring her feelings of fear onto you. She will suddenly feel that closeness to you is terrifying and that you are putting her in mortal danger by staying with her. Her fear, which was acquired in some previous frightening incident, attaches to you because your child can't do battle against abstract ghosts of the past. She does battle against *you*. You are close enough, safe enough, dedicated enough to stand by her while she fights against whatever force once frightened her into submission. If you allow her to struggle, cry, and tremble, without responding in anger, you speed her recovery from that terror.

This is a very tricky situation to handle. On the one hand, we must not overpower or manipulate our children. When we unilaterally force them to do our bidding with our superior size and strength, we do real damage to them. On the other hand, a child does not heal from fear unless a safe, aware adult stays close enough to allow the child to feel afraid as she perspires, cries, and trembles fear away. While we are learning to listen to fear, it's best to proceed a small step at a time. When your child begins to feel afraid, move gently to embrace her. If she screams and runs away, approach her again, slowly and reassuringly. At some point, she will start to scream, tremble, and perhaps lash out angrily at you. Contrary to all appearances, at this point you can be pleased. The discharge process has begun. You need not move closer quickly: you have reached a good balance between offering closeness and listening to her fears.

• **Explain to your child why you are staying close to her.**

Your child will ardently wish that she didn't have to feel her fears. In order to indicate to her that you are actually thinking about her, rather than simply making her life harder, you will need to explain now and again why you are staying close. The more fully you can give her your perspective as counselor, the more she'll be able to trust that you are thinking about her. So, why are you staying close? You are staying close because you want to be right with her when she's afraid. You stay because you know she is in no danger. You stay because you want to be with her when it feels like the worst things are happening. You love her and won't leave her to feel afraid by herself. You'll think of your own reasons as you learn to trust this process of healing fear. Your explanations won't stop your child from feeling afraid. They will begin to make sense to her after she has unloaded enough fear to realize that she is safe in your arms.

• **If your child is struggling against you, protect yourself from harm.**

As your child struggles with feelings of helplessness and terror, don't expect her to be "polite" or "nice." She can't be. She depends on you to realize that she is fighting her fears, not intentionally insulting you. In her fear, a child will fight vigorously; if you remain caring, she will tremble, perspire, and struggle for quite some time. Try to find ways to reach out and embrace her, while protecting yourself from her frantic motions. If she moves to hit, meet her arms with a shielding hand, or bend so that her fists land on your back or shoulders where no harm can come to you. If she is kicking, you might want to bring her gently into your lap and remove her shoes so her feet hit the carpet and not you. By permitting this struggle, you allow your child to powerfully vanquish feelings of helplessness. And by protecting yourself, you ensure that she won't feel guilty about this necessary struggle. You give her the chance to safely fight her way through a scary time, rather than whine, feel victimized, or retreat into passivity.

A child who has faced terrifying situations will fight with what looks like fierce determination to hurt the safe person helping her. It is possible to develop the ability to listen and be tender while at the same time quickly and firmly keeping yourself safe. If a child is trying to pull hair or scratch, you will need to hold her hands gently but firmly away from your face, letting her know that you will hold her hands only as long as she is trying to hurt you. She can continue to work through her fears, struggling in a safe way against whatever loose confines she makes necessary.

- **Reassure your child that the present is free from danger.**

As they discharge fear, children often re-experience parts of the incident that terrified them. Children who had breathing difficulties at birth often feel like they can't breathe again; indeed, they may begin to cough and become congested for a time. Children who suffered early injury or surgery might feel that your touch is unbearably painful; children who were threatened by an adult or sibling will feel sure that you are mad at them and ready to hurt them. Constant verbal reassurance helps a child as she works through fear. For instance, perhaps your child becomes afraid that she can't breathe, and later, afraid because her body is so hot. (In the discharge process, children put out great amounts of body heat.) You might say in a steady voice, "I'm right here by your side. You can breathe just fine. I'm watching every breath, and I'll make sure you don't stop breathing. I won't leave you to fight this alone. I'm watching every minute to be sure you're okay. It's just me holding you. You're hot, but you're okay. You'll cool down later. I'm going to put my hand on your head to help cool you down. Whatever scared you is over now. Nothing can hurt you with me here by your side." Your tone of voice is important. Your words are a steadying force, but a calm, confident tone carries far more reassurance than the words themselves.

Don't expect your reassuring words to soothe your child. Once she has plunged into working on her fears, your words and tone signal to your child that you aren't afraid. This will provide the contradiction that makes it safe for her to continue to work. The more confident you sound, the more panicked she can feel. If your reassurances accurately address the incident the child is working on, she will cry and tremble intensely. For example, one two year old I know tripped and fell over a toy. When his mother came to his side, he began fighting her with loud cries and eyes shut tight. She told him she would stay with him and talked to him in a reassuring way. He grew more fearful, active, and loud. He began kicking and screaming, "Pick me up! Pick me up!" His mother picked him up and held him in her lap. He kept screaming for her to pick him up, perspiring, and pumping his legs up and down in her lap with his eyes shut tight. He was wild with feelings. After five or ten minutes of this, it occurred to the mother that six months ago his face had been cut in a fall, and although she was with him when the doctor stitched him up, he had been strapped down for the procedure. She said to him, "I'm sorry I couldn't pick you up in the hospital. I wanted to pick you up. I've got you now, and you're safe. I'm sorry, sweetheart." His eyes flew open, and he looked directly at her, then clung to her tightly, trembling and sobbing intensely as she repeated her apology for another fifteen minutes. Her accurate reassurances let him work deeply to erase his fear.

• **Continue to move toward embracing your child.**

Your child will need you to gradually and thoughtfully move toward a full embrace. You need move closer only a bit at a time, saying what you are going to do before you do it. "I'm going to put my hand on your forehead now, love. I know you're scared, but it's just my hand." Sometimes, as you say what you are going to do, a child becomes intensely afraid of the simple movement you propose. When the mere thought of you moving closer helps her struggle and perspire, keep telling her what you want to do, but do it ever so gradually. You might take ten minutes to actually touch her forehead, holding your hand in her view while she trembles and cries as if it were a terrible threat. It is very useful to a child to have this kind of safe pretext as a focus for her fears.

The longer your child struggles, trembles, cries, and perspires, the clearer it will become that she is working through past fears. She won't tell you, "Oh, now I get it! I'm safe in your arms and I'm remembering when I was born and I couldn't breathe at first!" But her attention as she struggles against you will gradually shift from fear of you to the feelings she had in the incident she is working through. She will progress from saying, "You're awful, and I want you to get away from me," toward "I can't breathe, Daddy, I'm not getting any air! Oh, help! I'm not breathing at all!" (Meanwhile, she takes in fine large breaths.) "I can't get my breath! Help me! Oh, I'm scared!" While remembering this fearful time, she'll need you with her, body to body.

Often, at the end of a significant piece of work on fear, a child will make a transition from feeling fear to feeling relief and closeness to you. She will relax in your arms and sob fully as she realizes that you have been through her worst feelings with her. Hold her tenderly. She is feeling close to you, relieved, and deeply understood. It is a significant time in her relationship with you.

After working through fears, children need time to rearrange their perceptions of the world again. It looks and feels like a different place now that there is less to fear. You will see your child quietly watching, listening, and touching with a new awareness. She may just want to look at you and touch your face for several minutes, or she may fall into a deep sleep in your arms after a relaxed cry and some yawns.

- **If at any point you become afraid or angry, stop trying to assist your child.**

It is important that we try to help our children with their fears only when we are reasonable ourselves. When we become afraid or angry, it's best to stop and say, "I can't help you with this anymore. Let's both get up now—I can't listen any longer." It's very important to keep our children's trust by not pretending to be their counselor when we are confused or angry. Be forewarned, however, that once a child has started working through her fears, it's hard for her to stop in the middle of the process. If you have to move away abruptly, it may take her a while to return to her normal self. She may continue to find reasons to be upset, angry, or afraid, hoping you'll return to help her finish the job she started.

Because a child's fears feel so compelling, and because we tend to get angry easily when there is open struggle against us, the role of counselor to a child's fears takes time and practice to learn. You may notice that you can be supportive until she insults your parenting, which makes you angry, or until she looks at you in panic, which makes you panic, too. Getting regular Co-Counseling sessions about what triggers *your* fears or anger will help you navigate ever farther into this uncharted territory. Counseling a child on fear requires that parents wrestle with raw feelings, both their children's and their own.

WHEN CHILDREN AVOID THE THING THEY FEAR

When your child runs to you and tries to hide herself from a scary situation, your role in getting the discharge process started is straightforward. First, ensure her safety. Remove any real threat. Then gently encourage her to face the situation which frightened her. Asking her to look at the person or thing she fears, or to get a little closer, might be a good first step. If a child is stiff with fear, you'll have to retreat to a safer distance before you ask her to look. You may have to nudge a bit, lifting her face out of your lap or scooting both of you just an inch or two closer. You are trying to strike a delicate balance: loving attention and safety plus a dash of what feels to the child like danger. If you show too little warmth and acceptance ("Come on now, walk right up to that doggie. Let's go!"), a child feels forced to behave and can't freely shed her fears. If you provide too much sympathy ("Come here, honey. That's a very scary big doggie. We'll go where there are no doggies."), a child doesn't have the backing she needs to face the feelings of fear that need to bubble up in order for recovery to occur.

One child in my day care center became afraid every lunch time. She wouldn't sit down to eat and was very upset when offered any food except milk and Cheerios. She would be quiet and withdraw to the other side of the room when it was time for a hot meal. To start her recovery from her fears, all that was required was that a caregiver she trusted go to her, gently put an arm around her, and suggest (not demand) that she come to lunch. As she felt the slight nudge toward the table, she would begin to scream, protest, and perspire. When she would stop to look around after some minutes of panic, her caregiver would say, "Can we go over to the table now?" and nudge her again in that direction. She would focus again on her fears. Sometimes, we had to bring her to the table against her will, because a caregiver was needed with the other children. She could tremble and cry quite well on the caregiver's lap while lunch proceeded for the other children. After many full lunch-time panics, she began to be able to laugh about trying to touch her food, and at last, she began to voluntarily sample and eat foods she once was not able to look at. We never knew how her fear of food began, but we did succeed in helping her dissolve it.

LAUGHTER HELPS CHILDREN DISSOLVE FEARS

If your child's fear is not too overwhelming, you can begin to help lift it by encouraging her laughter, which releases the lighter tensions caused by fear. Your child will laugh if you can be comically afraid of the thing she fears at a time when she does not feel threatened. When you act afraid in a goofy, playful way, your child will be able to laugh heartily, over and over, and will probably join into the play in the powerful "I can tell you what to do and you have to do it!" role. This new power balance—the big person scared and helpless, the little person bold and masterful—is such a relief from a child's daily experience that laughter rolls plentifully as tensions ease.

One six year old I know was afraid to make telephone calls. All his friends used the phone easily, but he would always ask his mother to make calls for him, with a whine in his voice and a "hangdog" look. One day, when he and his mother were at home alone together, she brought the phone down onto the floor where he was playing and said with exaggerated insecurity, "I have to call Mary, but I don't think I can do it! Oh, dear! I wish I didn't have to!" She began to dial, but slammed the receiver down in a panic. "I can't *do* it!" By this time, her son was curious and amused but was not yet laughing. She kept going. "Oh, how can I do this? I won't know what to say!" She started to dial, screeched, and flung the receiver out of her hand like a hot potato. At that point, he laughed heartily. The mother continued her "chicken-hearted" monologue, being sure to fling the receiver away often, since that seemed to be the key to much laughter. After a while, he began directing her: "Pick it up, Mom. Come on, you *have* to call her, *now!*" Eventually, she dialed seven digits, pretended to begin a conversation, and then hung up in a panic. More hearty laughter. Her son began to deride her, "Mom, you are so dumb! Can't you even talk on the phone?" He would hand her the receiver, and she would throw it down in fear. Much laughter and some roughhousing ensued, as Mom tried to crawl away from her task and her son laughingly dragged her back to the telephone amidst her pitiful protests.

After twenty minutes or so of animated play, Mom said she had to get on with her chores and stopped the game. Twice more in the next week she found time to play the "telephone game," looking for the places that made her son laugh and elaborating on those themes. She said nothing serious or instructive to him about making his own calls. A couple of days after their third "telephone session," her son asked her for his best friend's number. She asked him if he wanted help making the call. He said no, that he wanted her to go in the other room while he made it himself. She went and listened from a distance while he made his first independent phone call.

This mother's game illustrates a general point: children can laugh their way toward increased confidence. Children love to play games in which they are the swift, the brave, the sure, and the adult is the slow, the timid, the befuddled. The laughter and permission to romp freely permit children to get a taste of power and to discharge the stored tension they've collected as denizens of a big, noisy, surprising, adult-paced world.

This type of play often gives your child a way to present and work through her more deeply-rooted fears. For example, perhaps your daughter has been jumping on you to try to ride you like a "horsie," laughing merrily as you gently shake her off and try feebly to get away. The game has been going on for twenty minutes or so. She lightly bumps her knee on the carpet—clearly, not a bad bump. But she looks at you with hurt and blame in her eyes, clams up, and rolls away from you. She lies there, remote and still. As you gently hold her and encourage her to look at you, she starts to scream and kick as if you were hurting her. She has used the safety of the wonderful game you were playing as her springboard into a session on her tougher fears. This leap from laughter to tight feelings of fear is almost always sudden. It baffles parents, who try to curtail active play before it gets to this productive but difficult stage. We have children who are eager to do the work of discharging their fears and who sense a prime opportunity when we play freely and thoughtfully with them.

FEARS IN THE NIGHT

Many children have trouble going to sleep at night, or awaken fearful before morning arrives. A good way to begin to heal bedtime fears is to have lots of active play, with laughter and roughhousing (no tickling) that allows the child the upper hand, before bedtime. This brings you and your child into close physical contact, which is a prime source of reassurance for children. It also lets your child feel understood: children feel very close to adults when play and laughter are at the heart of their time together. When it's time for bed, your child will have much easier access to the fears and other feelings that interfere with her sense of safety. She may start by protesting her bedtime, or by refusing to brush her teeth, or by insisting that story after story be read. Simply be pleased, confident, and keep heading in the bedtime direction. "I know you don't like it, Celia, but it's time to hop in bed, now." "Let's turn your body toward the bathroom, where your little blue toothbrush is!" "I've read three stories. We'll have to save that one for tomorrow." Once again, you want to provide safety with your warmth, together with a little nudge toward the thing your child fears.

At some point, your child will be able to break into struggle, perspiration, and frightened crying. Whatever the triggerpoint is, keep a light finger on it: if your child cries and struggles against moving toward the bathroom to brush her teeth, hold her and remind her now and then, "It's still time to walk to the bathroom and get ready for bed, Celia." If she screams and grasps at you when you move your arm to leave after cuddling in bed, hold your arm a bit away, so she can feel the impending separation (as well as the safety of your other arm, tucked around her body). If you focus on "getting the job done," getting her teeth brushed or the painful separation over with, these times of working through fear will irritate you greatly. To counsel a child on her fears, we adults have to relax our immediate timetables. The work takes time and effort, but it eventually frees you and your child from dependence on long bedtime rituals which only temporarily placate a child's underlying fears. Work on bedtime fears also seems to improve a child's overall sense of safety in the world.

One couple, after spending two hours each night for months trying to soothe their three year old to sleep, decided to help her wrestle with her fears. They cuddled with her, told her they were going to get up and go in the other room, and moved away just enough to start her crying. If they held her too close, the crying and struggling would stop, so they held her gently about a foot from them so that she could see them. She struggled, cried, and perspired mightily for almost two hours. They were exhausted. At last, her frightened look cleared, she asked for a kiss from each, then said she wanted to lie down. They tucked her in and stood in her doorway for a few moments while she fell asleep. They were very worried that they had done her harm. When her mother picked her up from day care the next afternoon, the caregiver, who had not been told about the previous night's doings, came up to the mother and said, "Cora was extraordinary today. She was so friendly, so outgoing, so thoughtful of the other children. We've never seen her this sure of herself!" She had a few more short cries at bedtime during the next few weeks but was able to relax and go to sleep far more quickly than before.

When your child wakes in the night terrified, you can help her make significant gains in undoing the fears that seize her. The biggest problem with night terrors is that we parents aren't at our most attentive in the wee hours of the night. Your child is ready to struggle, perspire, and cry away her fears, and she needs only your presence to keep the process going. If she's having a nightmare, it's often helpful to turn on the lights, or take her to a lighted room, so that when she regains consciousness she'll know where she is. Don't worry too much about waking her out of her dream. She'll awaken when she's been able to fight her fears long enough. In a way, the dream is useful to her. It provides access to the feelings of fear, which bubble up and then discharge through trembling and perspiration.

Paying attention to your child's fears during the day with laughing games and permission to tremble and cry will help resolve some of her nighttime fears. However, it seems that children address certain of their fears only when their conscious guard is down, during sleep. You may find, if you sleep with your child, that she sometimes perspires or trembles noticeably during the night. This is the healing process at work—without lots of help from you, for once.

WHEN FEAR CAUSES AGGRESSION

Sometimes children mask their fears. They feel uncomfortably distant and alone but can't think of how to help themselves. In this state, they behave normally as long as they can and then suddenly hit another child, pull little sister's hair, or start to lash out at you. These aggressive moments are like the plague to parents. They are easily misunderstood as intentional acts of meanness and they drive a wedge of irritation between parent and child. We feel, "Why doesn't she know how to control herself yet? She's already __ years old!"

Whatever the number of years people have lived, when they are afraid, they can't think. When children are too afraid to think, they act out the things that have hurt them. So if your child has been pushed on the playground, she'll be inclined to push someone when she is tense or afraid. Children who have been called names or who have seen others hurt by name-calling will, when tense or isolated, call those names, whether they understand the words they're using or not. Fearful incidents reprint themselves in a child's behavior in a very literal fashion.

To help a child work on fears that make her lash out, a parent must anticipate the trouble, get there before the hurtful deed is done, and step in to prevent harm. If you move in after one child has hurt another, the aggressor usually feels so guilty she can't show any feelings at all. She won't feel safe enough to cry effectively or to tremble her upset away.

Every child gives some warning signals that her fears are getting the best of her. It will take some investigative work to pinpoint these warning signs. Watch and listen carefully. The following are some of the signals I remember from particular children I have known: "When Mommy spends the evening away from home, Joey will bite other children at day care the next morning." "When other children sit close to Carol for longer than a minute or two, she will hit or kick them." "When Bobby comes home after school and slams the door behind him without looking at anyone, he will start insulting his little sister within ten minutes." "When toddler Jenny is left in the presence of a baby, she can be tender for about half a minute, and then she begins to poke and jab." "When Nathan walks into nursery school late, he immediately starts calling children names."

Once you know the warning signals, lifting fear from the child is a matter of being there to add your warmth and attention to the situation as it ripens. You want to allow the child's fears to rise to the surface where they can be felt and discharged. So you stay warm and close, perhaps right next to the child you expect will lash out. At the same time, you are on the alert to protect others from being victimized. When she finally leans over to bite, or reaches out to pull hair, or begins to kick, you stop the action gently but firmly. Bring her into your lap, or catch her hand on its journey toward little brother's hair, or hold her leg so she can try to kick, but no one is touched. You needn't say much. Perhaps you say, "I can't let you hurt Danny." "Looks like you're wanting to bite. Come onto my lap for a moment." "I'm going to hold this leg so it doesn't hurt Manuel." If your voice is steady and matter-of-fact, a child won't be frightened by your distress and can concentrate on her own. When she feels like hurting someone but is prevented from doing so without blame or upset, your child will be able to feel and work through the fears that cause her to lash out. She will try to struggle away from you or will simply burst out with upset. If she stays stiff and remote, warmly encourage her to look at you and to tell you what's bothering her.

One toddler at my day care center would inevitably bite other children when he hadn't seen his mother the night before. Since she attended regular classes, we knew exactly which mornings to expect him to be fearful enough to bite. He would enter the room somewhat quiet and withdrawn on these days but would say goodbye without clinging and start to play. We learned to have a caregiver greet him warmly and then stay within two feet of him so that when he lunged for a child's arm, she had a good chance of stopping him before he made contact. She would slide an arm around his tummy so he couldn't reach any farther and bring him over to her lap. He would squirm and look away. If she talked gently to him, saying, "Joey, I'm sorry you don't feel so well this morning. I can't let you bite Annie. Tell me what's got you upset," he would cry and struggle to get away, perspiring and working through his fears. If the caregiver had to leave him partway through to attend to another child, he would sit on the floor looking forlorn. When she returned with warm words and the reassurance of her embrace, he would struggle and cry some more. We found that if he could work in this way on his fears and sadness for about fifteen minutes, he would emerge more cheerful and would usually be able to make it through the morning without biting. If we couldn't give him enough time to work, or if we were so peeved that he couldn't find the safety to cry, the biting behavior would surface again and again. Over a period of many months of short opportunities to work through his fears, he grew gentler, trusted us more, and was more easily able to simply cry when he was upset rather than storing tension until he had to lash out.

LISTENING TO A CHILD'S FEARS
IS LIKE WALKING A TIGHTROPE

Almost no parent has ever seen another adult listen to a child work through her heavy fears. What we have seen is harshness, humiliation, or rejection aimed at children whose fears have overcome them. "Stop all that fuss right now or I'll tan that hide of yours!" "Come on, don't be a baby. You go into that classroom now or I'll tell the teacher you want to stay home and be Mamma's boy!" "Every time you hit your sister, I'm going to put you in your room and shut the door. That'll teach you!" It takes time, practice, and lots of support to step away from our habits of punishing children when they act out of fear. We are reaching for the ability to help them shed their fears, to dig out the root cause of their timidities and their aggressions. Like tightrope walkers, we must balance ourselves carefully against the pull of old habits. We inch forward on a totally new trust in our children's recuperative powers: when they lie cradled in our arms, feeling deeply afraid, we listen. We stay with them through the feelings, holding them gently until they rediscover their sense of safety. Then, across the wire at last, we watch as they enjoy their world again, less afraid and more powerful than before.

For most parents, to learn this kind of listening requires repeated conscious effort. We have found over the years that parents who want to stretch their ability to listen do better when they are listened to themselves. Co-Counseling sessions and parent support groups that meet regularly are both effective sources of support. They provide parents with a chance to think things through, ample time to discharge about common predicaments, and a chance to be reminded of how deeply each of us cares about our children.

REACHING FOR YOUR ANGRY CHILD

THE CHALLENGE

When our children are angry, we parents are thoroughly challenged. The intensity of their feelings is great, and we feel strongly in response. We often try to "talk sense into that child" at first. Reasoning with them rarely solves the problem, though, because children are trapped by their angry feelings. Their usual intelligence and good judgment are temporarily, but totally, disabled. They can't listen to or make sense of what we say. Our own frustration rises when they won't budge from their "impossible" position. Our own restimulation intrudes when our children are angry.

How do we turn angry times into constructive times? How can we begin to undo the distance anger creates? What's needed is a way to bring our angry children back into good communication with us. We want to let them know they are cherished even though things don't always go the way they want. If we reach out to an angry child, offering attention and love, she has the opportunity to fight through her resentment and do away with it. The alternative is to punish or isolate the child, who then stores up her anger inside, where it tends to grow and fester.

Handling children's anger is one of the most difficult and universal jobs in parenting. The information and practices presented here are based on the observation that when children are feeling upset or out of touch, they will recover their sense of well-being if allowed to discharge: to cry, tremble and perspire, tantrum, or laugh. Discharge expels the hurt and, if the parent stays close, clears the way for the child to feel competent and loved again.

NOTE: Before continuing, please read the other five chapters: "Special Time," "Playlistening," "Crying," "Tantrums and Indignation," and "Healing Children's Fears."

To make progress during angry times, we parents can lay important groundwork by establishing "special time" with our children. "Special time" works as an antidote to the crisis times that worry us. It allows our children to communicate with us on *their* terms and in *their* way. As we pay attention to them, finding ways to let them laugh and explore, they gain confidence that we are on their side. They can tell that we love them just as they are.

When we were angry children, most of us were treated with disrespect. If we were fortunate, we were sent away to cool off without physical or verbal abuse. Many of us were not so fortunate. Our parents couldn't tolerate our anger; they were too upset to help us through our troubled times. Because this intolerance for anger is our heritage, an overview of anger may be useful.

ANGER COVERS DEEPER HURTS

An angry child is one who is quite frightened and sad underneath her tough stance. However small the issue, she feels that something absolutely vital to her is being threatened, and she has no choice but to fight. She also feels alone. As far as she can tell, no one understands her, no one will come to her rescue, everyone is out to hurt her. Children naturally lean toward affection and companionship. When you see a child fiercely attacking her loved ones, you can assume that she is sitting on extremely painful feelings. She puts up her guard, daring us to care that she is hurt and needs help.

When children feel sad, they can discharge the hurt by crying. When they are afraid, they discharge by crying, trembling, and perspiring. When they are frustrated, they tantrum their way back to satisfaction with their lives. These recovery processes can be relied upon to restore a child's ability to love, reason, and and learn. However, there is no distinct recovery process that heals feelings of anger. Anger is the barbed wire fence we parents have to crawl through to reach a child who is frightened and full of grief. Once we learn to work our way toward our children while they are angry, we can assist them to shed the grief and fear that lie at the heart of the matter.

A CHILD'S ANGER ALWAYS HAS A FEARFUL EXPERIENCE BENEATH IT

When children feel they are in danger, are left alone too much, or when they witness other people being hurt, strong fears overtake them. During these hurtful times, they are almost always too frightened or overwhelmed to fight for themselves. An all-out fight would be a healthy reaction to danger, but if the fear is overwhelming, it makes children passive. They withdraw or freeze, and quietly try to survive. These frightening times make a deep impression. Children remain frightened long after they have reached safety. **They retain fear both of the particular trouble they faced,** *and* **the passivity that overcame them.**

To picture what these fears feel like, try to remember the worst nightmares you have had. Most of us have had dreams of needing to escape from a terrible fate, and not being able to make our bodies move, or of crying out for help, but having no voice. This frightening combination of danger and helplessness is something like the fears many children carry.

Small incidents can restimulate your child's fear from some long-past but genuine crisis. She feels just as alone and frightened as she did during that time of real trouble, but now that the *present* threat is minor, she defends herself at last. She gets angry. If she is a toddler, another child may sit too close to her, and she reaches out to pull his hair. Or, with an older child, a friend may tease a bit, and your child responds by starting a fistfight. Of course, the child's reaction doesn't make sense any longer—the real crisis is over. The angry child is fighting an unseen adversary. Her fears still haunt her, turning harmless incidents into replays of that old crisis. Telling her there's no need to be angry has no effect on how she feels, as you have surely discovered. But you can help her *work through* her fear and sadness by staying with her when her anger rises.

AN ANGRY CHILD CAN'T TELL YOU
THE REAL SOURCE OF HER FEAR

A child can't tell you, "I was afraid for my life just like when I got stuck in the birth canal for three hours." She will simply show panic or outrage whenever another child crowds too close to her. She won't say, "I feel scared, the same way I did when I cut my head last year." But when you try to help her with her scraped knee, she'll kick you and demand that you leave her alone. Real crises deeply affect a child, and they are recorded in detail in her mind, but are not always accessible as conscious memories. It is usually impossible for a child to refer directly to a crisis. Instead, the leftover feelings poke into your child's everyday experience like thorns into the flesh, causing your child to react angrily, even at times of warmth and closeness. You may not ever learn what originally frightened your child. Fortunately, children don't need us to completely understand their inner workings. They simply need our attention while they discharge the feelings that drive them "off track."

YOU WILL BE THE "TARGET"

When you attempt to reach past your child's anger to offer her support, you will see and hear about some long-fermented aloneness. Your child either couldn't get the help she needed at the time of crisis, or she was so frightened that she couldn't feel the help that was there. In either case, a frightened child feels alone against the world and terribly disappointed in *you*. It's unfair and irrational, but it seems that when children have felt endangered and helpless, they direct their reaction—usually anger and mistrust—toward the people closest to them.

Of course, you don't deserve to be the target of all that bitterness. You have done your level best to be loving, kind, loyal, and generous. Your child yells that you have never cared about her, you've been mean and thought only of yourself. It's no picnic reaching out to an angry child. But if you get busy defending yourself and straightening out "the truth," you won't be concentrating on your frightened child. She needs to tell you just how far away from you she feels before she can let you help her with her fears. Listening to passionately felt bitterness while you continue to offer your caring seems to be the fastest, most efficient way through the tangle. Remember, your child is frightened and sad inside and wants to find some way to trust you again so she can finally sob in your arms and feel your protection, your love for her.

YOUR GOAL IN REACHING PAST ANGER

Your goal is to lovingly stay with your child in spite of her anger, her intense desire to be alone, and her mistrust of you. An angry child is trying hard to discharge some deep hurt, but she doesn't feel loved enough to do so. You can't *make* her feel loved, but you *can* persistently offer your caring until that hurt has been discharged. After screaming, trembling, perspiring, and crying—the messy activities that relieve children of their deepest hurts—your child will be surprised and relieved to find that you've been on her side the whole time she's been angry with you.

YOU WILL NEED HELP

When reaching out to an angry child, a parent needs presence of mind, plenty of time, and faith that a tender heart can be found inside this furious young person. It also requires some skill you can only get with practice. No parent has these resources on hand every time her child's anger wells up, and few of us have had much practice in this area. Handling anger is like learning to juggle flaming torches: it's best to juggle easy items first, then try the torches, then add the flame. Start by listening when your child is crying and there is no anger involved. You need to get the feel of helping her through her grief, and she needs to learn to trust you when times are hard. Then, try staying calmly by during her tantrums and listening through her fears so that you gain an understanding of these recovery processes, too. You'll need to see that a sweetly reasonable child will emerge from a writhing, heated, seemingly out-of-control state. By now you may have built enough trust between you to add the flame: you can begin reaching past her anger.

Grown-ups in our society are understandably poor at reaching out to an angry child. Most of us were physically threatened or attacked (spanked, beaten, or belted) for angry behavior. We lose our cool around anger, because that's how our parents handled it. Those of us who struggle with our children's tight, angry episodes deserve consistent help to untangle our upsets from theirs.

Getting help for ourselves is a key step in reaching for our angry children.

Our own angry responses, like our children's, guard the door to feelings of sadness and fear. We are bothered by the heat of our own anger, fears that we've failed, fears that our children will fail, or fears that we won't survive the stresses of parenting. Search out a Co-Counselor who can be a caring listener. Talk about yourself, your child, your hopes, and your disappointments. You'll need a close counseling relationship to give you the safety to discharge fully on how hard it gets. A regular chance to discharge on your own upsets will give you more listening room for your child and more staying power as you try to reach through to her when she's angry.

GUIDELINES FOR REACHING FOR YOUR ANGRY CHILD

Here are some guidelines that can help you find your way past your child's anger to the healing of the fear and grief beneath.

- **When your child seems angry, stay with her and learn what you can about the nature of the trouble.**

"You took my last fish stick, and I wasn't even finished yet!" Your first job in an "angry" situation is to listen and sort out what is happening. Fresh indignation and tantrums are each loud, but quite different from anger, which tends to be tight, threatening, and mean-spirited. It can take a few minutes to understand whether your child is indignantly righting a wrong, beginning a healthy tantrum, or putting up a shield of anger. (Sometimes, a child will begin with indignation and get trapped in tight anger after a few moments.)

Stay close and encourage your child to tell you more: "What happened?" "Tell me more," "What is it that you want?" If you see bitterness, a tight, mistrustful tone, or a desire to hurt you or someone else, your child's guard is all the way up. If, however, she is angry but is already crying, perspiring, or trembling, the discharge process has begun. She is already using your assistance to make progress.

- **Assess your own state of mind. Are you level-headed enough to try to reach for her right now?**

When your child gets angry, it's wise to check your store of free attention. Do you have some time? Can you decide not to be upset with her for being angry? Are you ready to weather a difficult time in order to help her? If so, proceed.

If you feel attacked or enraged, your attention is on your own feelings and not on the needs of your child. At the moment, you cannot help her. It probably makes sense to try to break the grip of your own anger. Call a friend, or find a place—perhaps the bedroom, washroom, or garage—where you can yell, stomp, and pound on something unbreakable. When no counselor is available, noise and motion may help you regain some ability to think constructively again. If you can cry or tremble, some of your own tension will drain. One mother I know would lock herself in the bathroom when her fury was high. She would look at herself in the mirror, pound on the sink, and yell to herself that she was a good mother who didn't deserve all this trouble. She could cry hard for five or ten minutes about how hard her life was and come out much relieved, ready to attend to her children without anger. We mustn't pretend to reach out to our children when we're seething inside. And it's best that we aim our upsets in a harmless direction when we ourselves get too hot to handle.

As we try to reach out to an angry child, we need to promise ourselves that we will change course whenever we ourselves get angry. When we start to snap back or argue, it's time to take a break or to quit. Simply say, "I can't help you right now. I don't want to fight with you. I'll be back when I'm not so mad." When your anger flashes quickly, it's all right to just get up and leave the room. Explain later, after you've stomped around in the other room awhile. Our children can learn to make do while we aim our own anger elsewhere. These emergency procedures will help ensure that the mistakes you make as you learn will be shortlived.

- **Offer your child warmth and closeness. Don't force it, but do keep offering.**

Try to "hang in there." An angry child needs to discover that she won't lose your caring. You are trying to move toward her in spite of her attacks by showing that you want to be with her and that she matters to you. Discharge of grief and fear can begin when she understands that she can't get rid of your caring, no matter what she says or does. You need to listen fully to her feelings and not back away from her because of them. As you hold out your arms to her or reach to touch her gently, she will become dead sure that you are the last person on earth she wants to be with right now. She will fight you verbally, at least, telling you awful feelings she has about you. "I hate you!" "You're always making me feel bad!" "You never listen, and you're not listening now!" "You're making me even angrier! Just get away!" are the kinds of things you can expect to hear as she fights to keep the lid on the hurt beneath her anger.

- **Stay with your child, and keep listening.**

Your child may try to run away and be alone. She will tell you that's what she needs and that you are making her angrier by following. You'll be on shaky ground here, because none of us is an expert at remaining thoughtful while someone is acting as though we are the enemy. Also, there *have* been times when you haven't listened to her, and she is certainly reminded of them now. Your task is to stay close enough to let your child feel your attempt to help and to indicate that you are indeed considering what she says. This may mean, if you are being ordered to "Go away!" that you say, "Okay, I'll take a few steps back now, but what I really want to do is to come and sit by you on the bed."

The situation is paradoxical. Our children are trapped by deep feelings of hurt and don't feel safe enough to trust us in any direct way. Fairly or unfairly, they blame us for their troubles and can't stand to be around us. Yet, in spite of our shortcomings, we are at the moment the safest, most committed people in their lives. We are also the only people smart enough to reach out to them in times of trouble. In a way, when our children direct anger toward us, they dare us to come and find them. If they had given up on our love, they would be resigned and withdrawn, not engaged in heated battle. An angry child commends you in a backhanded way: your medal is inscribed, "Safe Enough To Get Mad At."

- **Explain to your child why you intend to stay.**

Your child needs to hear why you intend to stay with her after she has begged you to leave her alone. You need to be brief but informative. Be forewarned that the reasons you give will be understood only after her anger is over. To a child in the midst of anger, *nothing* makes sense.

Why do you stay with her? You stay because it hasn't helped her get over her anger when you've gone away before, so you've decided to stay with her this time. You stay because it seems to you that she shouldn't have to be alone when she's feeling so badly. You stay because, even though it feels awful to her, if you leave she might think you don't really care about her. You stay because you love her and want to be close when times are hardest. What's important is that you tell her, in any way you can, that you are trying your best to love her well.

- **If your child struggles against you, protect yourself as necessary. If you can, stay with her and let her continue to struggle.**

When you gradually, thoughtfully move close to an angry child, she will often try to fight in the same way she needed to during an earlier, genuine crisis. It seems that a child who has been terrified simply cannot sit and calmly cry about the time she felt deeply threatened. She never wants to go passive in her fear again, and, because you are "hanging in there" as a safe, tangible target, she can cast you in the role of the threat she once faced. It *helps* your child to struggle with these feelings of being victimized and unloved. This is usually the crux of reaching your child: your caring as she struggles almost always unlocks the tears and trembling that will bring her close to you again.

- **Don't allow your child to destroy valuables or to hurt anyone else in her anger.**

Children who are trying to get rid of their upsets don't want to hurt anyone. They don't *want* to be allowed to ruin things. A smashed Kleenex box or ripped magazine is nothing to worry about, but don't allow a child to ruin things you or others value. She will only feel guilty later. You must step in and, without hurting or lashing out at your child, prevent harm from being done. Pull a kicking child away from her sibling, hold firmly onto the toy she is about to throw, or hold her in your lap to keep her from ripping up the leaves of the potted plant she wants to destroy. Let your child show how upset she is and let her use her strength as she fights, but step in to prevent her from doing actual damage.

• **Resist the temptation to lecture, scold, or criticize.**

Your child cannot reason in the midst of anger. Anything you do to try to show that you're "right" and she's "wrong" will only prove to her that no one cares about her. If she became angry because of a reasonable position you took ("You must wear your bike helmet when you ride," or, "I won't let you watch this program on TV"), it's not the time to talk extensively about your reasons. Simply hold your position, love her, offer your caring, stay with her, and let her struggle through this irrational storm. If you can be warm and gentle, she'll eventually tremble, cry, and relax enough to remember that you love her. Once she's regained contact with you, her judgment will improve, and you can discuss things sensibly. Most likely, by this time your lecture about right and wrong won't be necessary. Your caring will have come through, and the importance of the issue will shrink back to realistic proportions.

Here's an example of how reaching for an angry child can work. In this family, there are two sons, twelve and fourteen years old, and a single mom. The younger son often feels competitive with his older brother. Their birthdays come three weeks apart, and birthday time is always a bit touchy because the older boy's comes first, leaving the younger boy vulnerable to feeling second-rate. This particular year, the mom remembered that the younger son would be sensitive, so on the older boy's birthday, she asked the younger boy exactly what he wanted. She wrote down everything carefully, including a request for the same kind of desk chair she had given the older son that day.

When the younger son's birthday came, that desk chair, in a different color, was her featured gift to him. He was furious. "Why did you give this to me—I didn't want it! Did I ask for a desk chair? Huh? Mom, you are so disgusting! You don't even think of me at all! You only think of Randy, and you get me the thing *he* wanted. You don't even care enough to get me something for *me*! This is the worst birthday I've ever had!" The tirade went on for quite a while. Her son stomped off into one room, then another, and then tried to throw the desk chair over. His mom, who followed him from room to room, held onto the chair so he wouldn't break it. She told him once, quietly, that he had asked her for a desk chair. She apologized, saying at various times, "I'm sorry you don't like it." "I wanted to get you something really great. It's your birthday, and you're very special to me." "I love you very much, and I wouldn't hurt your feelings for the world if I could help it." "I'm sorry if I made a mistake." She gradually moved toward him, and he sat down on his bed. She sat on the floor next to him and rested her arms on his leg. From that spot, she figured, he would see her looking into his eyes at least in his peripheral vision.

He finally could begin to cry as she said, "Pete, you've been special to me since the day you were born. I was so happy to see you that day, I felt like flying. You were beautiful to me then, and you are just perfect to me now." He reached out and put one hand on her shoulder, and she got up, sat next to him, and held him close. He cried harder. After a while, she asked, "Do you want me to tell you more about how I loved you when you were a baby?" He nodded, and they lay down together, his face turned toward the wall, and he cried off and on as she held him and told him other happy memories she had of their times together. After a half hour of crying and snuggling, he got up and had a snack. A while later, he came to his mom and told her that he liked the chair just fine after all and that he was glad she'd gotten a blue one because that color looked good in his room.

This mom recognized that the feelings behind her son's anger were old feelings—feelings she had anticipated. She had done all she could to make things right. She tried not to feel too badly about choosing the "wrong" gift, realizing that this was an upset that was, in an odd way, constructive. If Pete could cry about not being special, then she would have a chance to help him clear away another chunk of a misperception that bothered him often. She figured that if by tomorrow it was still the wrong gift, she and Pete could go do something about it. For the moment, she concentrated on listening, moving closer, and, little by little, finding ways to get her love across. She kept her attention on the important issue, her love for him, and didn't get too distracted by his angry motions, his insults, or his disappointment.

THE ISSUE OF VIOLENCE

Reaching past a child's anger to help her with her fears often means staying with a struggling or fighting child. Many people think that when a child begins to fight, someone should stand back and order her to stop: a child should not be allowed to be violent. This is almost correct. The child *does* need to be prevented from doing harm to others. But the child, overwhelmed with feelings, is not able to obey spoken orders, which usually only add fuel to the fire. Decisive (but not harsh) intervention by an adult is far more effective. The grown-up holds onto the book that's about to be hurled, puts an arm around the waist of the child who is flailing, untangles fingers from the hair of a sibling. After damage control, the child will benefit greatly if the adult is willing to allow her to continue to struggle against her fears so she can cry, tremble, and perspire until she's rid of the hurt.

All children start out knowing that violence is not a way to solve problems. When, in their anger, they attempt to hurt their friends, their siblings, or you, they're making a clear plea for intervention and help. An angry child who is hurting someone wants an adult to step in and provide enough resistance that she can struggle without being squelched or humiliated. She is trying to finish an important battle that she once lost. She wants to overcome the fear and self-hatred that drive her to lash out.

THERE'S TIME TO MAKE MISTAKES AND TO LEARN

Don't be upset with yourself if you make lots of mistakes as you try to handle your child's anger with this new approach. The idea is simple, but our children's upsets do rub our fur the wrong way. It's so tempting to hurl insult for insult, or to argue our well-reasoned positions.

Remember to bring your feelings and experiences to a Co-Counseling session so you can think, plan, and get things off your chest in preparation for the next angry episode. This will help ease some of the loneliness of parenting through hard times. With dependable assistance, it will become easier to reach for your angry child. Slowly but surely, you'll develop the powerful ability to brave criticism and struggle in order to restore the sense of love between you and your child.